Fellowship with God

FELLOWSHIP
WITH
GOD

Martyn Lloyd-Jones

LIFE IN CHRIST □ VOLUME ONE

STUDIES IN 1 JOHN

CROSSWAY BOOKS

A DIVISION OF GOOD NEWS PUBLISHERS
WHEATON, ILLINOIS • CAMBRIDGE, ENGLAND

CREDO
PUBLISHING CORPORATION

Fellowship with God.

First U.S. edition published 1993 by Crossway Books, a division of Good News Publishers, 1300 Crescent Street, Wheaton, Illinois 60187.

Published in association with Credo Books, P.O. Box 3175, Langley, B.C., Canada V3A 4R5.

Cover illustration: Keith Stubblefield

First printing, 1993

Printed in the United States of America

Library of Congress Cataloging-in-Publication Data
Lloyd-Jones, David Martyn.
    Fellowship with God / Martyn Lloyd-Jones.—1st U.S. ed.
        p.   cm.—(Studies in I John ; 1)
      1. Bible. N.T. Epistles of John, 1st—Sermons. 2. Sermons,
English. 3. Fellowship—Biblical teaching—Sermons. 4. God—
Love—Sermons. 5. God—Worship and love—Sermons. I. Title.
II. Series: Lloyd-Jones, David Martyn, Studies in I John ; 1.
BS2805.4.L58 1993   227'.9406—dc20   92-21507
ISBN 0-89107-705-7

01	00	99	98	97	96	95						
15	14	13	12	11	10	9	8	7	6	5	4	3	2

First British Edition 1992

ISBN 1 85684 063 8

Production and Printing in the United States of America for
CROSSWAY BOOKS
Kingfisher House, 7 High Green, Great Shelford, Cambridge CB2 18G

TABLE OF CONTENTS

ACKNOWLEDGEMENTS

As usual, these sermons were edited by Christopher Catherwood, the Doctor's eldest grandson. But as with all the sermons published since the death of Dr. Lloyd-Jones in 1981, a major role was played by the Doctor's eldest daughter, Elizabeth Catherwood, who in her capacity as literary executrix went through all the editing to make sure that it was fully in accord with what the Doctor would have wanted had he been alive to supervise the work. Special thanks are therefore due to her for all her hard work, and also to Alison Walley for copy editing the manuscript and for putting it onto disk ready for the publisher.

1

The Christian and the World

And we know that we are of God, and the whole world lieth in wickedness [or, in the wicked one].

1 JOHN 5:19

I begin our series with this verse because it seems to me to provide us with the background and setting to the teaching of the whole epistle. It is an epistle which, in many ways, people find somewhat baffling and difficult to understand. There are many reasons for that. Its message is essentially a very simple one, but the manner and the style of the writer, the Apostle John (for I take it that he was the author, we need not discuss that), this style, which is so characteristic of him, is one which, unless we are careful to maintain a firm grip of the great principles of his teaching, may very well cause us a certain amount of confusion. Never perhaps is it so true to say of any epistle that we are in danger of missing the wood because of the trees than it is in this particular case.

Some people have said that his style, or method, is kind of spiral; it seems to go round in circles and differs with every turn until he arrives at his ultimate truth and message. It is interesting to contrast the style of the Apostle Paul with that of John. The main difference is that John is not so logical; he is not so clear-cut in his method. He has, of course, exactly the same message, but he states it in a different way. It is said sometimes, loosely and lightly, that John was more mystical than Paul. I cannot admit that, because both of them were, in the truest sense, Christian mystics, but John's style is more indirect than that of the great Apostle who is always much more direct and logical in his presentation of truth. But, of course, there is a real advantage in having these different styles. Were they to do nothing else, they would remind us of what the Apostle Peter calls 'the manifold grace of God' (1 Pet 4:10), the many different colours. The light of truth is like the natural light; it can be broken up by prism into a large number of subsidiary colours which together form that perfect light. And so it is with the Scriptures, all from God, all in-breathed by the Holy Spirit, all perfectly inspired, and yet differing in these many ways, and thereby reflecting different aspects of the one glorious, ultimate truth. There is a unity, a wholeness about it all.

Another difficulty in understanding the writings of John arises, perhaps, from the fact that when he wrote this, the Apostle was undoubtedly very old. It is agreed by most that this letter was probably written somewhere between A.D. 80 and A.D. 90—you may take A.D. 85 as being perhaps a fairly accurate date—and by that time the Apostle had become an old man. Many things show that: we find him, for instance, speaking of his 'little children', and he uses very affectionate terms. There again, we find another difficulty arising, in that as he is saying one thing, it suggests another thought to him, so he immediately expresses it, and then comes back to the original point he was making. So it is important that we should bear the great central principles in mind, and here in this nineteenth verse we get the essential background to a true understanding of this letter: 'We know that we are of God, and the whole world lieth in wickedness', or 'in the wicked one'.

In other words, the theme of this epistle is the position of the Christian in the world. I always feel that there are three verses in the whole epistle which I would describe as key verses, and this is one of them. The second is chapter 5, verse 13: 'These things have I written unto you that believe on the name of the Son of God; that ye may know that ye have eternal life, and that ye may believe on the name of the Son of God.' And the third is chapter 1, verse 4:

'These things write we unto you, that your joy may be full.' There we have the great and grand objective which was in the mind of the Apostle. The theme is the Christian in this world, what is possible to him; how is he to face it; how is he to stand up to it; what must he do; what is his relationship to this world in which he finds himself?

Now the Apostle, writing as an old man, was addressing people who were in a very difficult world. I do not know how you feel, but I always think that, in and of itself, is a profound source of comfort. Half our troubles arise from the fact that we always seem to think that it is only our world and time that has been difficult. But if history, and the study of history, especially as we find it in the Bible, does nothing else for us, it should always give us a true perspective. When you look back across the story of the Church and of the saints you find that the world has often been as it is today. In a sense we are confronting nothing new at the present time. It has all happened before, and, thank God, there is provision here for us in our perplexities and in our difficulties.

That is why I cannot understand anyone who does not see the utter uniqueness of Scripture; it does not matter at what period of history you may happen to live, nor what may be happening in the world around and about you, you will find that the position has been met and catered for and dealt with somewhere or another in the Bible. And here is a letter written to people who were in an extremely difficult and contradictory world, and the old man, feeling perhaps that his time was short, is anxious that these little ones, these beloved children and grandchildren of his, should know what to do in such a world with all its contradictions and troubles and problems.

Now I do not need to point out how apposite all this is at the present time. I suppose that this is the biggest and most difficult question in many ways that those of us who are Christians today can possibly meet. What is our position in this world? How are we related to it? We are in the same world as everybody else and we are subject to the same things as they are. We do not live enchanted lives; we are all here in the flux of history, and the great question is, what are we to do; what is the difference between us; how are we to adjust ourselves; what is to be our attitude towards current events and affairs; what is our duty with respect to life in this world, and how are we to conduct and comport ourselves?

Those are the great questions that are considered in this epistle. It is by no means the message of this epistle only; indeed a very good case can be made for saying that that is precisely the message of nearly all the New Testament epistles. And in the same way, of course, the book of Revelation was written to comfort and strengthen the first Christians. It was written to people who were suffering persecution and hardship, and it was meant to enable them to overcome their immediate difficulties, as well as to give them a general view of the course of history in the years of the centuries that lay ahead. So let us first look at this message of this epistle in general, before we come to divide it up into its component parts.

Now a time of difficulty and danger is often a time of panic, and there are many ways in which people can show this. It is not only thoughtlessness, alas, because thought can equally be a manifestation of panic. Indeed, even prayer may be a very striking manifestation of panic. Sometimes, panic can be mistaken for true spirituality and a true understanding of the scriptural teaching. But while the effect of the New Testament teaching always is to steady us—and it steadies us of course by presenting us with the truth—it never makes a mere general statement, it is never out just to soothe and comfort us for the time being. No, its message always is that there are certain great principles, and that if we only lay a firm hold upon them and grasp them, if only we base our life upon them and plan the whole of our existence in terms of them, then we can never really go wrong.

Therefore, in a situation of difficulty and of crisis, the first thing we must do is to make sure that we have grasped the New Testament teaching. I do not want to be controversial, and I am particularly anxious not to be misunderstood, but if I may put it in a phrase, in order to call attention to what I have in mind, I would say that in a situation of crisis the New Testament does not immediately say, 'Let us pray'. It always says first, 'Let us think, let us understand the truth, let us take a firm hold of the doctrine.' Prayer may be quite useless and quite void. The Bible has a great deal to tell us about prayer and as to how it should be made. Prayer is not a simple thing in one sense; it may be very difficult. Prayer is sometimes an excuse for not thinking, an excuse for avoiding a problem or a situation.

Have we not all known something of this in our personal experience? We have often been in difficulty and we have prayed to God to deliver us, but in the meantime we have not put something right in our lives as we should have done. Instead of facing the trouble, and doing what we knew we should be doing, we have prayed. I suggest that at a point like that, our duty is not to pray but to face the truth, to face the doctrine and to apply it. Then we are entitled to pray, and not until then.

I mean something like this: if the whole attitude of the Christian in any situation of crisis or difficulty were just to be immediately one of prayer, then these New Testament epistles with all their involved teaching would never have been necessary. No, the New Testament method says, 'You must become certain people before you can pray. There are certain preliminaries to apply, and you must know what you are doing when you pray.'

Now that is something that surely we too need to be very clear about. We need to apply certain great central principles and truths and these are the very things with which John is concerned in this first epistle of his. Therefore, as we look at it we shall be impressed by certain things; we shall be impressed by his realism and by the way in which he does not attempt to gloss over the difficulties and to make light of the problems. Thank God, the Bible always faces things as they are, even at their worst. That is why to me a psychological use of the Bible is of the devil. It is a mis-use of it, because the Bible is not concerned simply to ease a situation. It has a strength and a power; it is concerned about courage, but in terms of its own truth so it looks at the world as it is, at its worst. People say, 'Why, that is depressing!' Well, if it is depressing to you, it is because you do not accept the teaching of the Bible. To be realistic should not be depressing to those who think straightly and clearly, and this is a realistic book.

And then the other great thing that characterises its message is the way in which, having looked at the facts and having faced them squarely and honestly, it applies quite clearly its own great and glorious remedy. And in this verse which we are now considering we are reminded of some of the great characteristic notes of this particular epistle. Firstly, you will find that we come across these words: 'We know.' Then, secondly, we find something about ourselves—that we are of God. And, thirdly, we are told that there are certain things that are always true about the world.

The first thing then, is this great certainty—'*We know.*' John has written these things that they may know that they have eternal life. We need not stay with this, and yet, of course, it is something which is absolutely basic, for this meets the whole position. Christians are not people who are in a state of uncertainty; the very definition of Christians in the New Testament is of people who know where they are, what they are and what they have got; they are not men and women who are hovering in the dark.

Perhaps the days and times through which we are passing are, in that sense, a great advantage to us. There are many senses in which I thank God I am preaching now in this pulpit today and not one hundred years ago or at any time during the nineteenth century. It was so typical of that century for people to talk about the quest for truth and all the excitement that accompanied that quest. You see, in days when life was smooth and easy, then people said how exciting it was to investigate truth and to examine it, and there were people who thought that that was Christianity. It was to be 'a seeker', and you read literature and you compared this with that, and you said how marvellous it all was! But in a world like this of the twentieth century you have no time for this, and thank God for that! We are in a world where black is black and white is white and that is in accordance with the New Testament teaching.

Christians are men and women who are certain, and John writes in order that these people may be absolutely sure. They were sure, but there were certain things that were not clear to them. That always seems to be the position of the Christian in this life and world. We start with the truth which we believe by faith. Then it is attacked and we are shaken by various things but, thank God, these lessons are given to us to strengthen and establish us. That is the first thing to be emphasised in this message, and it is something of which we may be sure. There are certain things that you and I should *know*. Christians have ceased to be seekers and enquirers; they are men and women who have ceased to doubt.

The whole doctrine of assurance and salvation has been heartily disliked in the past hundred years or so. We have heard very little about it and people have thought that it was an unmentionable item. There have been many reasons for that; there is something which can be objectionable about a certain kind of person who claims this knowledge. It can be said in a way that is antagonistic, but that is not what we are commanded here. No, the whole glory of the Christian gospel is that it gives us knowledge; it claims to be the revelation of God; it gives that unique and definite authority, and Christians should know exactly where they are and how they stand. They should have been emancipated and delivered out of the realm of tentative conclusions. There are certain absolutes and we shall see how the Apostle keeps on repeating these. There are certain things possible to you; you must get hold of them and you must hold fast to them.

But about what are we to have this certainty? Firstly, we are to be certain about ourselves. We know that we are of God. What is a Christian? Are Christians just people who pay a formal respect to God and to public worship? Are they just mechanically attached to a church? Do they just try to live a good life and to be a little bit better than others? Are they just philanthropists, people who believe in a certain amount of benevolence? They are all that, of course, but how infinitely more! Now, says John, we know this truth about ourselves as Christians. 'We are of God'; by which he means nothing less than this: we are born of God; we are partakers of the divine nature; we have been born again; we have been born from above, we have been born of the Spirit, we are a new creation.

Now those are the basic postulates of the New Testament position. May I put it like this. I cannot see that the New Testament message has any comfort to give us or any consolation unless we start from that basis; that if we are Christians we are altogether different from those who are not. We know that we are of God—children of God, related to God in that intimate sense, receivers of His very life and nature; in other words, the whole point about Christians is that they are unique and they are aware that they have this new life within them. Paul says, 'I know whom I have believed' (2 Tim 1:12); or he refers to 'the Son of God, who loved me, and gave himself for me', 'Christ liveth in me' (Gal 2:20); 'in Christ' (2 Cor 5:17)—these are his terms as they are the terms everywhere in the New Testament, and the Apostle John starts on this assumption—that we *know Him*. We are not just hoping or just trying to be Christians, it has happened to us, it has all taken place.

Here, then, is the question which we ask ourselves before we proceed any further—do we know that we are of God? Do we know for certain that God has done something in our lives? Do we know that something of the divine life of God is in us? Are we aware of the 'new man' within us, one that is entirely different from the 'old man' that we were by nature? Are we aware that there is something about us which we can only explain in terms of God? Can we say in true humility with the Apostle Paul, 'By the grace of God I am what I am' (1 Cor 15:10)?

Now that is absolutely basic and fundamental. Christians, according to this teaching, are those who have been called out of and delivered from this present evil world; those who have been translated from the kingdom of darkness into the kingdom of light, and who have been taken out of the dominion of Satan and translated into the kingdom of God's dear Son. There is no question about it; that is what has happened to them; that is what makes them Christians and they know it. They are able to say, 'I am aware of this life that is beyond me and within me, and I ascribe it only and entirely to the grace of God in Jesus Christ.' They are aware, not only of a difference between the world that does not believe in Christ, and themselves, but also of this difference between what they were before and what they are now. They can say, 'Though I am amazed and astounded when I consider the sins I have committed and all my unworthiness, I know, in spite of it all, that I am of God; God has had mercy upon me and has worked in me the miracle of the rebirth.'

The second thing we know is the truth about the world. 'We know that we are of God, and the whole world lieth in wickedness' or 'in the wicked one'. What he means by this is that it lies in the power of the evil one. Here again, as we shall see times without number in the study of this epistle, it was an essential part, not only of John's teaching but that of all the Apostles and of the first Christians with respect to the world. They drew this distinction between the Church and the world; the absolute difference between the Christian and the non-Christian; and the truth about the world, according to this teaching, is that the whole world lies under the dominion of Satan, in the grip of outright evil.

Let me emphasise this. The New Testament teaching is that however much the world may change on the surface, it is always under the control of evil and of sin. This admits that the powers of evil can be modified a great deal, and they have been modified during the passing of the centuries. Look back through human history and you will see that there is a kind of grouping. There have been periods when the world has been getting better, but these have been followed by a terrible declension, and the teaching of the New Testament is that the whole time the world has been 'lying in the wicked one'.

Now that is where, it seems to me, we have been so steadily fooled for the last hundred years; and when I say 'we', I mean the Christian as well as the non-Christian. How confident people were towards the end of the nineteenth century that the world was being Christianised! But we must not be deluded by all these changes which are merely superficial; the world, says John to these people, is under the dominion of Satan and sin, it is in the grip of evil, it always has been and it always will be.

And not only that, he goes on, as does the whole of the New Testament, to tell us something of the future of this world, and, of course, this is a vital part of our understanding of our relationship to the world. According to the New Testament (and here we get the realism) the world will always be the world; it will never get better. I do not know the future, there may be another period of apparent reform and improvement, but the world will still be 'lying in the evil one', and indeed the New Testament tells us it may 'wax worse and worse' (2 Tim 3:13). Indeed the evil of the world is so essentially a part of it and its life, that its final outlook will be judgment and destruction. You will find this teaching everywhere. The evil in the world cannot be taken out; it is to be destroyed; there is to be an ultimate climax and there will be a terrible end.

Now Christians start with that view of the world; they are not fooled by it, nor misled by it. The result of this is obvious— Christians have an entirely different view of the world from every other kind of person. Let me put it like this. Christians should not be at all surprised at the state of the world. If they are surprised at it, if they have been deluded by the apparent Christianising of the world in the nineteenth century, then they had better examine their Christian doctrine. No, what is happening today is a confirmation of the New Testament teaching; so Christians are not surprised at it; they do not expect anything different, and they are not, therefore, made unhappy by what they see.

Then, lastly, how are we to relate ourselves to all this? That is John's great message. Let me indicate what he does not say. Does he suggest we reform the world, that we set out to try and improve it—patently that is impossible! Does he, on the other hand, suggest that we turn our backs upon it and withdraw from it completely? Again he does not say that. What he does say is that it is the business of Christian men and women in this world first and foremost to make absolutely sure of themselves, that the world does not come in. They maintain their Christian position; then and then only they turn to the world. What do they do for this world? They restrain the evil as far as they can; they believe that that is God's will, so they pray to Him to have pity and mercy upon the world. But when they are praying they always remember that because of the evil of the world it may be God's will to punish it.

So Christians do not pray lightly and loosely on the assumption that if they pray for God to hold His hand then God will do that. No, the Old Testament has a great message with regard to that. There was a time when God said in effect to His prophets, to Jeremiah and Ezekiel, 'Stop praying for these people. If Daniel and Noah prayed for them, I would not do it.' That does not mean we do not pray, but it does mean that we pray intelligently and thoughtfully. It means that we pray as seeing God's ultimate plan for this world, and that all our prayers are subject to His holy will. The

Christian does not pray so much as a member of a country, but as a member of God's kingdom, as one of those unique people. They are of God, they are out of the world in that sense, yet they ask God to have mercy and compassion.

But, thank God, we are not left like that; we are told, and this indeed is the great message of this letter, that though we are in the world that lies in the wicked one, yet we may live with joy, we may be more than conquerors. There are certain simple principles which we must recognise and implement, and though things are as they are, we, with Christians everywhere, may have a full, abounding and complete joy.

2

Full and Lasting Joy

And these things write we unto you,
that your joy may be full.

1 JOHN 1:4

In our consideration of chapter 5, verse 19, we found that the real message of John's letter was the statement: 'And we know that we are of God, and the whole world lieth in [under the dominion and power of] wickedness, [or the evil, or the wicked one].' In other words, we must emphasise the fact that this letter has nothing to say to us unless we accept its definition of a Christian. That is the presupposition of all these New Testament letters; they are not written to the world, but to believers, to Christian people.

I emphasise this point because a failure to grasp it often leads to confusion. In the ministry of the Christian Church there are certain divisions which have, of necessity, to be drawn. The Church of God has a message to the world. To the unbelieving world it is an evangelistic message, and one of the great functions of the Church is to preach that message. But that is not her only message, for she has one for people who have been converted. She must build up the believers; she must talk to the saints and establish them in the faith and give them greater knowledge and understanding. Now if I may speak personally at this point, this is a division that I like to observe. I always preach on Sunday mornings on the assumption that those who are listening are Christians; it is a message to the Church and Christian people, and on Sunday nights my concern is to preach an evangelistic message. So that if there are persons present on Sunday mornings who feel that the message has nothing to give them, then I suggest that they should attend on Sunday evenings as well.

I make that point because of an experience I once had. I remember during a visit to Toronto that on my first Sunday morning, in response to a word of welcome, I announced that that was what I considered the right and wise thing to do. I said that I should be speaking in the morning on the assumption that everyone listening was a Christian and that in the evening I should speak on the assumption that people were not Christians, and that they were there to see how they might become Christians. An incident followed which I felt was significant in this respect. There was a lady present who only attended the services at that church on Sunday mornings; she had never been known to attend in the evenings. To the surprise of the minister, when speaking to him and myself as she left the church, she announced that she proposed to come in the evening. When the minister expressed his surprise, she said that she had now understood that she was not a Christian and would therefore come to learn how she might become one.

So, the basic assumption of this great epistle is that it is for Christians, and it is something which we shall have to hold in our mind constantly as we work through its message. As Christian people we are in a gainsaying, evil world. John has some very strong comments to make about the world in this letter. We must remember constantly that it is a very evil place. According to the Bible the whole mind and outlook of the world is opposed to God; it is under the dominion of Satan and in the grip of the wicked one. Christian men and women must realise that they are living in a world like that; that because it is a world that is opposed to God, it will be doing everything it can to drag them down. It will try to fill their minds here with things that will try to satisfy them and thereby keep them from God and Christ. It is a world in which Christians have to fight for their souls; it is easier to go down than to keep straight. 'We are of God, and the whole world lieth in the wicked one.'

But we see that the Apostle avoids certain errors as he goes on to tell us how we must relate ourselves to that. He does not tell us to start by trying to reform and improve the world. That is of course the tragedy, that so often the Church has imagined that that is her function. That has been the great trouble during the past years, since about the middle of the Victorian period when the Church became a kind of institution; when the line between the Church and the world became so vague as to be almost non-existent, and people talked about 'Christianising' society. There is nothing of that in the New Testament.

On the other hand we are not to turn our backs upon the world in the sense that we are to go right out of it. We are not told to become hermits or anchorites. That also has been an error, and it is very interesting, as you take the long story of the Christian Church from the beginning until today, to find how constantly those two extremes have been very prevalent. There have been those who have set out as Christian social reformers, and then there were those who said that was wrong and that the only thing was to go right out of it. That is the basis of monasticism, and the tendency is perhaps to revive that in certain forms.

But the teaching of this letter, as indeed the teaching of the whole of the New Testament, avoids both these errors and extremes; it is not a programme of world improvement, nor is it a programme of world renunciation. No, it gives us a picture of this kind of position in which we find ourselves, with this opposing spiritual force, this spiritual power that is represented by the world. Our fight is with that, and we are taught in this epistle that we can conquer it, we can rise above it, and we can defeat it, in spite of everything that is so true of it. In spite of the dangers that beset us on all sides, we can triumph and prevail; we can be 'more than conquerors'. And that is summed up very perfectly in this verse which we are now considering.

The Apostle now tells us, 'These things write we unto you, that your joy may be full.' That is it. That is what he is out for. He is anxious that these Christian people, to whom he is writing, should have fullness of joy, though they are in the world which lies under the power of the evil one.

Now that is the amazing thing which is offered us and promised us in the New Testament. It is by no means a message confined to this epistle. We see it in Paul's epistle to the Philippians: 'Rejoice in the Lord always; and again I say, Rejoice' (Phil 4:4). Our Lord promised the same thing in John 16:33: 'In the world ye shall have tribulation,' He said. He described the world as an evil place and He forewarned His followers what to expect from it. He said the world 'will hate you as it has hated me', but His great promise was that He would give them this joy that He Himself possessed. There was to be a period at the Crucifixion and before the Resurrection when they would be unhappy and miserable, 'But,' He said, 'I will see you again and your heart shall rejoice, and your joy no man taketh from you' (Jn 16:22); and 'These things have I spoken unto you . . . that your joy might be full' (Jn 15:11)—the very words that John repeats here.

This is His promise, and again let us remind ourselves that perhaps there is nothing which is more characteristic of the book of the Acts of the Apostles than this very note. There is no more exhilarating book than that; I always regard it as a kind of spiritual convalescent home, a book to which tired Christian people should always go to be really invigorated and built up. If you are feeling tired and therefore in need of a spiritual tonic, go to the book of Acts and there you will find this irrepressible joy that these people had in confirmation of the Lord's promise!

This is something that is very concrete and definite, which we are offered in the whole Bible. We see something of it even in the Old Testament Scriptures, in Isaiah and in the Psalms, for example. Christian people in this world are meant to be full of joy. That is what we are called to, and we are failing in our Christian witness unless we are experiencing and manifesting it.

What, then, is this joy? What does it mean? Well, first of all let me put it negatively. This desire of the Apostle that our joy may be full reminds me of certain things that are not to be true of us; let me note some of them. As Christian people we have no right to be in a state of melancholy or unhappiness because the world is as it is. Now you see where the background becomes so important, so vitally important. Christians are people, as we have seen, who, above all others, take a realistic view of life in this world; indeed, they should know more about it than anybody else.

Christians do not drug themselves; they are not like the people of the world who think that things are better than they are.

The first thing that must be true of Christian people is that they are honest and realistic; they do not look merely on the surface; they look beneath it. They do not always try to minimise their problems and make out that things are not as bad as they appear to be. They are not always clutching at various possibilities which are suddenly going to remove their troubles and problems; they do not buoy themselves up on various hopes. Christians have seen that all that is wrong; their knowledge of the Bible makes them certain; they have discovered that the world is an evil place.

So here is the danger; the danger confronting people who see things like that is to become melancholy and unhappy. It is the danger of saying that this life and this world are so terrible and hopeless, what can one do? Melancholy, morbidity, a sense of hopelessness and despair—many Christian people have fallen into that. But the person who is feeling melancholy is not one who is experiencing the full joy of the Lord.

In the same way we are not just to resign ourselves to the world as it is in its state and condition. The Christian is not in the position of just making the best of a bad life. There are many again who have fallen into that particular error also. They say, 'Yes, we see that we are not to be guilty of melancholy. Very well then, what is to be our position? Have we to make the best of a bad job and say to ourselves, "We are but strangers and pilgrims here," we have to put up with it for a few years, but we will soon be out of it and there it is?' But that is something which is quite incompatible with this New Testament concept of joy. A person who is resigned to conditions is not full of joy; yet we are told that that is what we should be.

In the same way, John is at great pains to emphasise that we should not be afraid; we must not be in a state of fear, because 'perfect love casteth out fear' (1 Jn 4:18). Paul, in writing to Timothy, said, 'For God hath not given us the spirit of fear; but of power, and of love, and of a sound mind' (2 Tim 1:7). Now it is very difficult for Christians not to be fearful in a world like this. They see the forces of evil; they are aware of the evil and the malignity; they are aware of their own weakness and they are afraid of this mighty power. We need not stay too much with these points, but I think that the kind of legalism that often enters into the life of Christian people is due to nothing but that very spirit of fear. I suggest to you that monasticism is finally based on the same spirit. A man says, 'I cannot stand up to these powers. The only thing to do is to run away from them.' And there are many kinds of monasticism in the spiritual world. People set their rules and regulations—you must not do this, but you may do that—and you live within a confined life. That is the spirit of fear, not the spirit of joy, for if we go through life and this world and are afraid of various things, then we are not filled with joy.

Or let me put it like this. The Christian is clearly not a person who practises what we may describe as a false puritanism, and I want to emphasise the word 'false'. We are not, in the words of Milton, to 'scorn delights and live laborious days'. We are not to give the impression that to be a Christian is an unhappy thing. Or, to sum it up finally, we are not to trudge along in this life painfully; it is a very easy thing to fall into these errors in a world that lies in the power of the evil one, but the very terms of John suggest an entire antithesis to all these things I have mentioned.

Let us, then, look at this word a little more closely. What is joy? 'These things write I unto you, that your joy may be full.' I can see what I am not to be, so what is our definition of joy? This is a question which appears to be simple at first, but the moment you consider it, it is extremely difficult. Can you define joy in a phrase or sentence?

Now it seems to me that we can do nothing better than what we find the Apostle Paul doing in 1 Corinthians 13, that great chapter on the theme of love. Why did Paul write it? The answer is, he had to write the whole chapter because he could not tell us in a sentence what love was. So in defining love he tells us that it does not do this, but it does do that; and the trouble with so many of us in these days, as the result of reading newspapers, is that we have developed small minds! No, these things are too big for that; you cannot define love in a phrase. You have to say quite a number of things about it and you find that you have not explained it even then. Paul, then, has given us a whole chapter on his definition of love, so I suggest to you that we shall have to say a number of things in an attempt to define what is meant by joy.

Another thing we must bear in mind, in any definition we may give of New Testament joy, is that we do not go to a dictionary; we go to the New Testament instead. This is something quite particular which cannot be explained; it is a quality which belongs to the Christian life in its essence, so that in our definition of joy we must be very careful that it conforms to what we see in our Lord. The world has never seen anyone who knew joy as our Lord knew it, and yet he was 'a man of sorrows and acquainted with grief'. So our definition of joy must somehow correspond to that.

Or take it in terms of some of His followers. The Apostle Paul was a man who knew a great joy even in prison. It did not matter where he was, it did not desert him, he was still joyful, and yet in our definition we must include this: 'We that are in this tabernacle do groan, being burdened', 'earnestly desiring to be clothed upon with our house which is from heaven' (2 Cor 5:4, 2). So we must bear those things in mind. The dictionary may say that joy is this, that or the other, but we must have a definition which will cover the joy which was experienced by these great exponents of the Christian faith and above all by our Lord Himself.

It is certainly not flippancy, not a sort of brightness which is overdone, not something which cheaply makes people laugh. I emphasise these negatives because we are such creatures of reaction. I think we all dislike heartily that kind of false puritanism to which I have referred, and it is agreed that there probably was a great deal of that in the Victorian era—the kind of people who said you should not lift the blinds on Sunday, for example, and who imposed some horrible regulations upon those who were trying to be Christians and even upon the children. But the tragedy is, that having seen that that was a false representation of Christianity, people have become a little too superficial. They have gone right over to the other extreme and have put on this flippancy, this superficial joyfulness, in order to say, 'I, at any rate, am not like those Victorians.' But we are not meant to be like this either. Let us beware of these things, let us go to the source itself. In other words joy does not mean lightheartedness, nor does it mean a pleasant emotional feeling.

These, then, are the negatives; so what *is* joy? I suggest it is something like this. The joy about which the New Testament speaks is never something direct and immediate. You cannot make yourself joyful in the New Testament sense; it is always produced by something else. It is a state which is the result of the interactions of various forces and factors playing upon the soul.

What do I mean by that? Well, here, I suggest, are elements of joy. Firstly, a state of complete satisfaction. There is no joy unless I am satisfied; if I am dissatisfied in any respect I am not joyful. My intellect, my emotions and my desires must be satisfied and, more than that, they must all be satisfied together and at the same time.

Let me illustrate that. There are certain things in this life and world which can give me intellectual satisfaction. Indeed, I may be perfectly satisfied intellectually, but my heart may be cold, and if that is so, then, even though my mind is satisfied, I am not in a state of joy. It is exactly the same with desires. There are things I can do which will satisfy my desires, but my mind and conscience condemn me; there is pleasure for the time being, but there is not joy. The satisfaction that is a part of joy is a complete satisfaction—mind, heart, emotions and desires; they are all fully satisfied, and full satisfaction is an essential part of joy.

But it does not stop at that; the next element in joy is a spirit of exultation. What would we say, I wonder, if we were asked to define the exact difference between happiness and joy? The difference, I would suggest, is that joy is more positive than happiness. Let me give you a simple illustration. Look at a little child sitting with its toy; there it is playing, and it is perfectly happy. Then suddenly you come along and from your pocket you produce a new present. The child springs to its feet; there is a brightness, a flush which is exultant—and that is the difference between happiness and joy. Joy is more active; the child was perfectly happy before, but now it is joyful; there is this positive spirit of exultation and rejoicing.

But I want to emphasise the third element which again to me is vital to a true conception of joy. I suggest to you that in joy there is always a feeling of power and of strength. That is why I was at pains to ridicule the false notions of joy; there is never anything flabby or superficial about it. Joy is one of the strongest powers in the world. Someone who is in a state of joy is, in a sense, afraid of nothing. When you are truly joyful, you are wound up by some mighty dynamic power; you feel strong, you are lifted up above yourself, you are ready to meet every enemy from every direction and quarter; you smile in the face of them all; you say, 'I defy them, they can never rob me of it.' The joy of the Lord is your strength; it is a strong power, a mighty robust thing.

There, then, is a very inadequate description and definition, and yet I suggest to you that we cannot get much further than these elements. Joy is something very deep and profound, something that affects the whole and entire personality. In other words it comes to this; there is only one thing that can give true joy and that is a contemplation of the Lord Jesus Christ. He satisfies my mind; He satisfies my emotions; He satisfies my every desire. He and His great salvation include the whole personality and nothing less, and in Him I am complete. Joy, in other words, is the response and the reaction of the soul to a knowledge of the Lord Jesus Christ.

And that is what we are to have. But let me emphasise two words—we are to have it to the limit. 'These things write we unto you, that your joy may be *full.*' Those of you who are interested in Greek terminology will know this word means 'filled full', and our joy in this world is to be full in that sense. Though the whole world lies in the wicked one, and though so many perplexing things are true about us and about our circumstances and conditions, our joy is to be filled to the brim, a real fullness without stint and without limit.

Secondly, 'These things write we unto you,' says the Authorised Version, 'that your joy may be full'; but a better translation would be this: 'These things write we unto you, that your joy may *remain* full', not only that it may be, or become, but that it may remain so. You see what he means? Not only while we are together worshipping God and singing His praises, but also should war come, should the atomic bomb descend, should I be thrown into a concentration camp, my joy must remain full. That is why we emphasised strength. I have not truly got the joy of the Lord if it is going to be variable and dependent upon circumstances and accidents and things that may happen to me. No, I say it is a deep, profound, dynamic thing that enables me to stand whatever may be happening to me, whatever may be taking place in the world, because I know Him, because I see Him and because I know that nothing can separate me from Him and from His love.

Christian people, have you got this joy? Do you know it; have you got this deep intellectual satisfaction; are your emotions satisfied to the full; is your every desire finding completion and all it asks for in the Lord Jesus Christ? That is what we are meant to know; that is what we are meant to have, and, thank God, this epistle has been written in order to tell us how to have it and to hold it, and that it may remain in us, come what may.

3

How to Know
the Joy

And these things write we unto you,
that your joy may be full.

1 JOHN 1:4

We saw at the beginning that 1 John is a practical letter. It is not a theological treatise, nor is it written from a theological or academic standpoint; it is meant to aid, encourage and establish Christian people. So we started with a consideration of the need to realise our basic position: that 'we are of God' and that the whole world lies in the power of the evil one. Then we saw that we should be experiencing a full and unshakeable joy, and so now the question is, how we are to have this joy and how we are to retain it. That was the question confronting those first Christians as it now confronts us, and the Apostle wrote his letter in order to tell them how this joy that is in them may remain full in spite of what may happen to them or come to meet them.

Now it seems to me that the right thing for us to do at this particular point, before we come to a detailed analysis of the letter, is to summarise its argument or message. We have seen that on the surface it is rather a difficult epistle because of its literary form and because of the characteristic mentality of the writer. But though his

31

method is spiral, with each circle leading on to the next, there is very clearly a scheme to be discerned in the letter. He did not write at random; these are not the mere ramblings of an old man; there is an order, if we will take the trouble to discover it. It is important, therefore, for us to have an analysis of the letter so that when we do come to the details we shall not be lost in them, but shall remember that the details are part of a great principle.

As we come, then, to an analysis of the letter, we come to something that is extremely interesting. It is a notorious fact (and this has always been agreed) that it is practically impossible to find any two men who have ever themselves agreed in their analysis of this particular epistle. There are people who are like gramophone records; they hear a certain commentator's analysis and they repeat it, but any man who thinks for himself generally ends by having his own analysis. It is very interesting to look at these authorities, such as they are, and to notice the various disagreements, but there are, at any rate, certain broad principles of classification which seem to me to give the best clue to the understanding of this epistle.

There is, I suggest, a division of the letter into three main compartments. The first division consists, in general, of the first three chapters; the second division consists of chapters 4 and 5 to the end of verse 12; and from verse 13 to the end of the fifth chapter you have the conclusion.

In the first division, the Apostle is laying down the conditions which are essential before this joy can be obtained and remain in us. In the second division, he then exhorts these people to practise the principles that he has already laid down, and it is at that point, perhaps, that these divisions of mine deviate most of all from most of the others. But at the beginning of chapter 4 he starts appealing to them: 'Beloved, believe not every spirit'; he is exhorting them, and from there on, as I want to show you, he continues with this exhortation. And then, having done that, he proves his conclusions from chapter 5 verse 13 to the end of the letter.

That is the fundamental division, but again that seems to be sub-divided in turn. Take this first great section in which he shows us what is essential before we can ever have and hold this joy. That now is divided up like this. The first thing is the absolute centrality of the Lord Jesus Christ. He starts with Him; the first three verses are devoted to a description of Him: 'That which was from the beginning, which we have heard, which we have seen with our eyes, which we have looked upon, and our hands have handled, of the Word of life; (for the life was manifested, and we have seen it, and bear witness, and show unto you that eternal life, which was with the Father, and was manifested unto us;) that which we have seen and heard declare we unto you, that ye also may have fellowship with us: and truly our fellowship is with the Father, and with his Son Jesus Christ. And these things write we unto you, that your joy may be full.'

Yes, but you will never know any joy until you know Christ. He is the source of joy; He is the fount of all blessings; everything comes through Him. So before John begins to discuss anything else, he talks about Him.

Here again we come to the great watershed which divides Christian preaching and teaching from every other teaching; it is based solely on the Lord Jesus Christ. The Christian Church has nothing to say to the world until it believes on Him. Indeed, the Church's message to the world is one of condemnation until it believes on Christ. Christ is central, He is essential, He is the beginning and the end, and John has nothing to say to these people by way of encouragement unless they are absolutely clear about Him. It is through Him that we have access to God; and it is through Him that we have fellowship with God.

So we start with that as a basic postulate, something that we do not even discuss; namely that if Christ is not the only begotten Son of God and our Saviour, in the way the New Testament indicates, then there is no Christian message and no joy and consolation. Then, says John, if you have believed on Him, the next great thing, in order that you may always have fullness of joy in this world, is that you have conscious fellowship with God—abiding in Him and He in us.

Now that is the great theme in this first section. You will never know this joy, says the Apostle, and it certainly will not remain full, unless you have this fellowship. But how is that to be maintained? John proceeds to deal with that from 1:3 to 2:28 and this is how he puts it to us. There are certain things that tend to militate against that fellowship and to rob us of it; there are certain things which will stand between us and that fellowship which in turn leads to joy.

First of all, there is sin—unrighteousness, and we shall see how he divides that up into committed acts of sin, and the refusal to acknowledge or confess sin. Those are the ways in which sin can come between us and a conscious enjoyment of the fellowship with God. John works this out in an extraordinary manner. He has told us about this possibility of great joy; then comes in a word which almost crushes us to the ground at once: 'This then is the message which we have heard of him, and declare unto you, that God is light, and in him is no darkness at all' (1:5)—and fellowship seems hopeless. But then, thank God, he tells us how it can be dealt with. If we do recognise and confess sin, then there is the blood which cleanses, and God is faithful and just to forgive us our sins (1:7, 9).

The second hindrance which John talks about in chapter 2 verse 3 is the lack of love to the brethren. If there is anything wrong in my relationship to God, I lose the fellowship and I lose the joy. Yes, but if there is anything wrong in my relationship to my Christian brothers and sisters, I also lose the joy and John works it out in a very subtle way. You lose contact with the brethren and you lose contact with God; you lose your love to God in the same way.

The third hindrance is a love of the world, a positive love for the world, a desire after, a hankering after its pleasures and its whole sinful mentality. This again is an interruption to fellowship with God. You cannot mix light and darkness, you cannot mix God and evil; therefore if you love the world you lose fellowship with God and again you lose your joy.

And the last thing which interrupts fellowship with God, he tells us at the end of the second chapter, is false teaching about the person of Jesus Christ. Obviously if the only way to God is through Christ, if I am in any way wrong about my teaching or my doctrine concerning Him, then automatically I sever the communion and again I lose my joy.

Those, then, are the hindrances—but thank God John does not stop at that. In the first section he tells us that there is a great source of comfort and strengthening: the unction of the Holy Ghost, an advocate within us, as well as an advocate with the Father, who opens our eyes to these things and forewarns us and shows us where we can get release and deliverance.

The second great essential to joy in this life and world is a conscious possession of eternal life. The first was a conscious fellowship with God; now it is a conscious possession of the life of God within us. That is the great theme from the end of chapter 2 verse 28 to chapter 3 verse 24. Again, he tells us, there are certain hindrances to this. In a hurried word he tells us something of what this eternal life within us means, and the hindrances to this are exactly the same things as before.

First is sin—a failure to keep the commandments of God will always rob us of our conscious possession of eternal life. When we live the godly life, we have this assurance and this happiness; but if we fall into sin, we begin to doubt and to wonder, and the devil encourages us in this. There is nothing that so upsets our assurance and confidence as sin; the same thing that breaks fellowship with God leads to uncertainty about the divine life within.

Then the second thing is lack of love to the brethren. He tells us exactly once more what this means and he works it out in detail. In effect he says, 'If you do not love your brethren, you will find that when you go to God in prayer, your heart will be condemning you and you will have no confidence in your prayer. It is interrupting your fellowship and communion and you begin to say, "Well, if I do not love these people who are Christians like myself, I wonder if I am a Christian."' A conscious possession of eternal life is essential to Christian joy, and a lack of love to the brethren again robs us of it because it creates these doubts within us.

And then the next thing once more is false teaching about the Lord Jesus Christ. If for a moment you become unhappy about your understanding of Him, if you once have false notions concerning Him, you immediately lose assurance of salvation; you lose this conscious possession of the life of God within you, and that is why John keeps on repeating these things.

So in a sense you have the three same obstacles as you did in the first section, but, thank God, once more he reminds us of the power of the Holy Spirit; 'He that keepeth his commandments dwelleth in him, and he in him. And hereby we know that he abideth in us, by the Spirit which he hath given us' (3:24). Thank God for the possession of the Holy Spirit who, when we are faced by these enemies which get us down, is always there to do His blessed work and will restore us. So that is the first section; those are the conditions which must be observed before we can have this joy.

We then come to the second section in which John exhorts us and appeals to us to practise these things in an active manner. We now have to apply what he has been laying down for us; that is the theme of the epistle from the beginning of chapter 4 to chapter 5 verse 9, and it can be summarised like this. First of all make certain of the spirits—'Beloved, believe not every spirit' (4:1)—make certain that the spirit within you is the Holy Spirit of God; make certain that you are not being fooled by some false spirit; that is the first exhortation.

Secondly, verses 7–21: make certain that you are dwelling in the love of God; that is absolutely essential. Everything you have got, says the Apostle, has come to you because of the love of God; so make certain you are abiding in and practising that love. Then, thirdly, make certain that you are actively keeping His command-ments and that you are overcoming the world that is opposed to you—that is the beginning of chapter 5.

And then, fourthly—you find this in chapter 5 verses 5-9—make certain that you hold right views of Jesus Christ and that you are in the right relationship to Him. Be absolutely certain about His person, because if you are not certain about Him, you will have nothing at all.

Then we come to the last main section. If you do all this, says the Apostle, this will be the result—chapter 5 verse 10 to the end—you will have the assurance that you are a child of God. 'He that believeth on the Son of God hath the witness in himself: he that believeth not God hath made him a liar; because he believeth not the record that God gave of his Son' (5:10). You do these things, says the Apostle, and you will have the witness in yourself.

And the next consequence will be that you will have confidence in prayer. 'This is the confidence that we have in him, that if we ask any thing according to his will, he heareth us' (5:14).

The third consequence is that you will have victory and conquest over sin and over the world; and the final result of it all will be that you will know in the very depths of your life and being that you are a child of God. Though the whole world may be rocking around about and beneath your feet, and though hell may be assailing you from every direction, in the confident, quiet knowledge that you are a child of God, you will have a peace of which nothing can rob you.

There, then, in outline, is the argument of the Apostle; that is the way in which we can obtain joy and maintain it in spite of everything. Now you observe that in doing all that, the Apostle is incidentally doing something else. As we work out this great argument, we shall find that, incidentally, we shall be coming face to face with some of the great central, primary doctrines of the Christian faith. Again I must observe that while this letter is not a theological or doctrinal treatise, it is nevertheless full of theology. These Apostles could never write a practical letter without being full of theology.

The New Testament is never concerned just to administer a little comfort to us; that is why we must constantly emphasise at the present time that psychology is often an enemy to the Christian faith. The only comfort is theological comfort, and notice how the Apostle deals with that in the letter. He starts with the great and mighty central doctrine of the Incarnation, but he is not finished with the first chapter, which is a short one with only ten verses, before he has also dealt with the doctrine of the Atonement.

Then he hurries on to the doctrine of regeneration and the rebirth—it is perhaps one of the classic passages and statements on the doctrine of regeneration in the entire Bible. At the same time he is dealing with the doctrine of sanctification—the third chapter has often been a great battleground for rival theories on this doctrine; but at the same time he has been dealing with the doctrine of sin and the doctrine of the devil. There is no clearer statement about the devil, the adversary of our souls, than you find in this epistle, and at the same time he deals with the whole doctrine of the Second Coming and the return of the Lord.

So in a very short compass we find ourselves confronted with
the great eternal principles of the Christian faith. It is like a mighty
ocean into which one can dive and swim knowing that one will
never cross the border with these great absolutes, with these things
that can never be moved, these absolutes in the realm of the spirit
and the eternal. In a changing world like this which is so shaky and
uncertain and where there seems to be no final principle on which
you can base your whole view of life, here we are in the midst of
the 'immensities and infinities', as Carlyle called them.

That reminds us, therefore, of the all-importance of theology,
of an understanding of the teaching of the Bible. God forbid that
we should be so interested in the words of the Bible as to miss the
Word itself, or that we should be so interested in our analysis that
we miss the message. The message is essentially theological and
doctrinal, and 'Apart from this doctrine,' says John, 'I have nothing
to give you, or to say to you because you will never know this joy
unless you yourselves are solidly based upon the foundation of
truth.'

That, then, is the great doctrinal language, but there is, however, one piece of background that is really vital to a true understanding of this epistle. John was not only writing positively, he also
wrote negatively, because there was difficulty in the early Church
at this time—about A.D. 85, you remember, towards the end of the
first century. So he wrote to build up these people, yes, but also to
warn and safeguard them against the subtle enemy that had
appeared, and he deals with it, in a sense, throughout the epistle. A
certain false teaching had come into the Christian Church even in
these early days. Let no one think that heresy and apostasy are new.
These things came into the Church before the end of the first century, and the Apostle speaks of one of the most famous of them,
which called itself *Gnosticism.*

This was a sort of admixture of philosophy and mysticism
which had become quite popular, and a number of these people had
become Gnostics and had brought this into the early Church. They
claimed to have special knowledge. They said that they had a
unique revelation, that they could enter into some mystic state in
which things were revealed to them that had not been revealed to

the ordinary person. That is the meaning of Gnosticism—a special knowledge, a peculiar understanding. They said, 'We special people have seen things, we have an understanding which no one else has got.' But it was really nothing but speculation and they speculated in particular with regard to certain doctrines.

This matter is not only dealt with here: it was the whole theme that the Apostle Paul was dealing with in Colossians 2. That is why, at the end of the chapter, he denounced that false asceticism which these people were practising. It was a contradiction of the Christian faith, but some of them had become deluded as a result of this teaching—you find it referred to in the epistle to the Ephesians also. It was, firstly, a false teaching with regard to the person of our Lord, so you see how essential it is to know this in order to understand John's epistle. It was a false teaching with regard to the reality of the Incarnation, and it really denied the doctrine of the God-man.

This is what it said—there were two views. There were those who said that our Lord did not really have a true body, but it was a phantom one. They said that the Word was not made flesh, but the Word, the eternal Son of God, came and put on a sort of phantom body, so that He never really suffered in the flesh on the cross. That was why Paul said, 'In him dwelleth all the fulness of the Godhead bodily' (Col 2:9)—no phantom body but a real one.

Secondly, there were those who said that we must always draw a sharp distinction between the man Jesus and the eternal Christ, and this is how they did it. They said that the eternal Christ came into the man Jesus when He was baptised of John in the Jordan. Then, they said, on Calvary Christ went out of the man Jesus and the man remained, so that Christ was not crucified; He certainly did not die for our sins, it was the man Jesus who was put to death on the cross.

That was the strange doctrine which was being taught with regard to the person of our Lord. Indeed, the first three or four centuries of the Christian Church were really spent in great councils arguing about the person of Jesus Christ—God-man, God and man—the reality of the Incarnation, and so on. So John deals with it here.

The second trouble about their teaching was that it was a false view of matter and therefore a false view of sin. It taught that mat-ter was essentially evil and that therefore anything that belonged to matter was in and of itself evil. It said that God had not made the world, because the world was obviously evil. So, how did this world come into being? It said that there were a number of emanations from God and that it was one of these emanations that had created the world. They also talked of various angels which came out from God, and that is why Paul denounced angel worship.

Now we must remember these things as we continue in our study of this epistle, but it worked out like this in practice. Regarding matter as evil in and of itself led to two reactions. The first was a sort of monasticism and rigorism which was designed to destroy the flesh. Paul argues against this, and John does the same thing. These people said that we must spend the whole of our lives in mortifying the flesh; the flesh is evil and therefore we must efface it, we must put on a camel-hair shirt, we must mutilate our body, in a sense, because the flesh is evil—monasticism—and this view has continued throughout the centuries.

The second reaction was quite the opposite to that; it was a sort of liberalism. These people talked like this. They said, 'The flesh is evil, but after all the soul is not in the flesh, so it does not matter what the flesh does. Therefore,' they said, 'there is no such thing as sin. I may do something which is wrong, but it does not matter, the flesh will be destroyed in any case and it is my soul which is going on to God.' That is what is sometimes called 'the sin of the Nicolaitans', and that is why John argues with such strength and force and power against this terrible teaching. These doctrines to John were so vital that he calls these teachers 'liars'. He uses some very strong language; he is the Apostle of love, but this view is so damnable, it is so inimical to the best interest of the soul. These men who do not accept the revelation, who claim such unique under-standing and initiation into the mysteries—they are of the devil, says John, they are liars and they must be denounced and avoided at all costs.

There is a great tradition that has come down through the ages that John was one day visiting a public bath, and as he was about to enter the water he saw one of the most famous of these Gnostic teachers coming out of the bath and he refused to enter—he would not bathe in the same water as such a man!

Here, then, is the emphasis of this great truth: the absolute centrality of true doctrine, the central importance of being clear in our view of the Lord Jesus Christ and His work. You cannot make short cuts in the spiritual life. If you desire to know this joy, if you are anxious to have it remaining in you whatever may happen in the world around and about you, there is only one way and that is to confront these great and glorious truths, to believe and to accept them and to avoid every subtle heresy, anything that would come along and put itself before us as human reasoning and understanding and philosophy. That is the way, says John, and thank God, He instructs us. There are certain absolutes—the Incarnation, the Atonement, regeneration, sanctification, the doctrine of sin and of the devil and the doctrine of the Second Coming. And as we believe and understand and practise these things in our relationship to God, in our relationship to one another as Christians, and in our relationship to the world that is outside, the joy will remain in us. Indeed, it will increase and continue, and at the end we shall find ourselves standing in His holy presence with joy unspeakable and full of glory.

4

The Apostolic Declaration

That which was from the beginning, which we have heard, which we have seen with our eyes, which we have looked upon, and our hands have handled, of the Word of life; (for the life was manifested, and we have seen it, and bear witness, and show unto you that eternal life, which was with the Father, and was manifested unto us;) that which we have seen and heard declare we unto you, that ye also may have fellowship with us: and truly our fellowship is with the Father, and with his Son Jesus Christ.

1 JOHN 1:1-3

We shall not deal with this entire statement now, but it is essential that we should read it all, especially the third verse, in order that we might have an understanding of the great message that the Apostle has to convey here to these Christian people to whom he is writing. They had their problems; there is nothing new in the difficulties of the world; it is always full of difficulties and problems. Indeed, our central difficulty today, perhaps, is to fail to realise that all our troubles are, in a sense, exactly the same as the troubles of mankind always in the past, and that there is a common origin of all these things. But it is a part of our human conceit to talk about the problems of the twentieth cen-

43

tury as if they were different from those of the first century—but they are not, they are exactly the same. There are differences, I admit, in the local or particular manifestation, but it is the cause of the trouble that counts.

In other words, the problem of mankind is similar to the problem of disease in our physical bodies. We may have one disease with a number of symptoms; they may vary very greatly from case to case, but it is not the symptoms that matter, it is the cause of the disease, it is the disease itself. Now that becomes important, because if we are only concerned with symptoms, we shall only be concerned with treating those symptoms and so we shall probably fail to apply the full message of the gospel. And yet the business of the Church is, in the light of these three verses, to proclaim, to announce the gospel of our Lord and Saviour Jesus Christ.

Let me illustrate what I mean. If I listened to the authorities, even in the Church, today I should be giving an address on the importance of the United Nations Association,[1] and how important it is for all of us to join it and to belong to it and to further this work. God forbid that I should say any word of criticism about the work of the United Nations, or the United Nations Association, but it is not the business of Christian preaching to recommend any such proposal for treating the symptoms of the disease. Our concern is to expose the disease itself, the thing that causes the trouble that leads to the necessity of the United Nations Organisation. That is the business of the gospel, not to be spending its time in treating the symptoms but to tell the world about the one and only remedy that can cure the disease which is the cause of all our local and particular troubles.

The first-century Christians, therefore, were face to face with the same thing as we are today. So the question is, what has the New Testament gospel to say to people living in a world like that? And we have already reminded one another of the answer. It is that in such a world and even under such conditions, it is possible for us to have a joy which is unquenchable, which cannot be defeated, which can prevail and triumph under any conditions whatsoever; a joy that can be brim full whatever these conditions and circumstances may chance to be. In other words, the message of the New

Testament is one which comes to individual Christians and to groups of Christian people in that sort of world. It does not tell them how the world can be put right, but it does tell them how they can be put right in spite of that world, and how they can triumph in and over it and have that joy in spite of it. As Professor Karlbach of Switzerland has said, 'It is not the business of the Church to try to discover world unity and order but to witness to the finished work of Christ'[2]—and that is precisely what we are now considering together in these verses.

Having then looked briefly at John's analysis of the whole epistle, we now come to look at it more in detail; and we must start, as John compels us to do, with the first three verses.

Here is the message, so let us analyse it by putting it in the form of some simple propositions. The first is that the gospel is a declaration, a manifestation, a showing. '(For the life was manifested, and we have seen it, and bear witness, and show unto you that eternal life, which was with the Father, and was manifested unto us;) that which we have seen and heard declare we unto you, that ye also may have fellowship with us: and truly our fellowship is with the Father, and with his Son Jesus Christ'—we *show* it unto you, says John.

Now he uses two words there which seem to me to bring us to the very heart of this matter. The gospel is an announcement. We can put that negatively by saying that the gospel of Jesus Christ is not a speculation, nor a human thought or idea or philosophy. It is essentially different, and it must never be put into that category. That is the trouble, alas, with so many of us. We will persist in regarding it as an outlook, as something which results from the meditation and thought of man on the whole problem of life and living. That has been the real tragedy of the last century or so, when philosophy took the place of revelation and people said that the Bible is nothing after all but human thoughts, man's ideas, man's search after God—why should modern man equally not have a place in these matters? So we put forward our modern ideas.

But that is not the gospel! The whole position of the Apostles, John and the rest, is that they have something to declare, something to say. They have seen something, they are reporting it, and that something is so wonderful that John can scarcely contain himself. Have you noticed the interesting point that in a sense there is no introduction to the epistle? There are no preliminary salutations and greetings; John does not even say who he is—you have to deduce that from internal evidence. Here is a man who has something amazing to say; he knows these people have to hear it and so, without any introduction, he suddenly plunges them into the heart of the mighty message he has to deliver. There is nothing uncertain about this message, it is a proclamation; there is an urge and an authority behind it.

In passing perhaps we should observe that it is the loss of this very note in the preaching of the Church, in this century in particular, that accounts for so much of the present state of the Church, and the present state of the world and of society. A man standing in a Christian pulpit has no business to say, 'I suggest to you', or 'Shall I put it to you', or 'On the whole I think', or 'I am almost persuaded', or 'The results of research and knowledge and speculation all seem to point in this direction'. No! 'These things *declare* we unto you'. I know that the old charge which has so often been brought up against the Church and her preachers is that we are dogmatic; but the preacher who is not dogmatic is not a preacher in the New Testament sense. We should be modest about our own opinions and careful as to how we voice our own speculations, but here, thank God, we are not in such a realm, we are not concerned about such things. What we do is not to put forward a theory which commends itself to us as a possible explanation of the world and what we can do about it; the whole basis of the New Testament is that here is an announcement, a proclamation—those are New Testament words.

The gospel, according to the New Testament, is a herald; it is like a man with a trumpet who is calling people to listen. There is nothing tentative about what he has to say; something has been delivered unto him, and his business is to repeat it; it is not the business of the messenger, first and foremost, to examine the credentials of the message, he is to deliver it. We are ambassadors, and the business of the ambassador is not to say to the foreign country what he thinks or believes; it is to deliver the message which has been delivered to him by his home government and the King he represents. That is the position of these New Testament preachers, and that is how John puts it here—'I have an amazing thing to reveal,' he says.

Now this applies not only to men who occupy Christian pulpits and have the privilege of doing so, it is something that clearly applies to all Christians. For as we discuss the world, and its present state and condition, with our fellow men and women, we are all of us individually to behave in the same way. We are to announce this, to proclaim it and not merely to put it forward as an ideas amongst others. All the Apostles did this. Read what the Apostle Paul tells the Corinthians about the way in which he came to them: '. . . not with excellency of speech or of wisdom, declaring unto you the testimony of God' (1 Cor 2:1). So the first thing we have to recapture at the present time is that, in the realm of the Church, we are doing something which is quite unique. It is unlike every other meeting. You have political meetings and people put forward their ideas; they certainly try to persuade us, and there are things they would have us believe. But there is not this finality; there are rival theories and possibilities. But in the realm of the Church we are out of all that, and we are concerned with a declaration and a proclamation.

It seems to me that it is beyond any doubt whatsoever that the present state of the Church is mainly, if not entirely, due to the fact that we ourselves have become uncertain of our message. Christian ministers have become uncertain about the miracles, uncertain about the supernatural, uncertain about the person of Christ. Hesitancy and doubt have come in, and at last this has become true of the common people everywhere, and there is a querying and a doubting. But the uncertainty began with the preaching, and once we cease to declare and to show, we have departed from the New Testament position. That then is the message for the Church herself at a time like this. She must cease to hesitate or to be nervous or uncertain; we are to stand by these things, and if we stand by them we need not consider the question of falling. The world may fall away from the Church, but let it do so, for she will have to listen again to the message; for the message is a proclamation. That is the first principle.

The second principle is that this declaration of the Church comes to us on the authority of the Apostles, and here again is something that is absolutely fundamental. Peter, in his second epistle, says: 'We have not followed cunningly devised fables, when we made known unto you the power and coming of our Lord Jesus Christ, but were eyewitnesses of his majesty' (2 Pet 1:16)—and that is exactly the same thing as John is saying here. Our only authority is the apostolic witness, and our gospel is based upon what they have said. In these three opening verses, John keeps on repeating it. Three times over he talks about having 'seen' it, twice he says, 'we have heard' it, and he also says, we 'have handled' it. Now he emphasises and repeats that because it is the whole foundation of the preaching of the Church, and there is no message apart from it. The message is what the Apostles have seen, what they have witnessed and what they have experienced and shared together.

Now, one of the first things we must recapture is the essential difference between witness and experience. What is our fundamental authority as Christian people? There are large numbers today who would say that it is experience. A man once wrote that he had been listening to a radio discussion between a Christian and a modern scientific humanist. During this discussion the scientific humanist asked the Christian, 'What is your final proof of the reality and the being of God?' 'And,' said the writer of this article, 'the Christian failed badly in my opinion. He tried to produce certain arguments, but he should have turned to the scientific humanist and said, "I am the proof of the being of God."'

But I would have been entirely on the side of the Christian in that argument, for I am not a proof of the being of God, nor is my experience. The only reality of the being of God is the Lord Jesus Christ. Experience is of value in confirming, in supporting, in helping me to believe these things, but I must never base my position upon it. Once I do that, I really have no reply to make to the psychologists who would explain the whole of the Christian faith in terms of psychology. I do not base my position upon my subjective states and moods and conditions which come and go and are so variable and changing. I have something solid, a solid rock. No, I thank God that I base my position upon certain facts in history: 'that which we have heard, that which we have seen with our eyes, which we have looked upon, and our hands have handled, of the Word of life'.

That is the basis, the apostolic witness and the apostolic testimony. If what we have reported in the Bible by those first witnesses and Apostles and others is not true, if their facts are not true, well then, I have no Christian faith, for to be a Christian is not to believe an idea, nor is it to undergo some subjective experience. All sorts of agencies can give experiences. There are many ideas which we can believe and they may do us a lot of good. The world has discovered that there are all sorts of psychological tests which people can apply to themselves. But that is not the Christian position. The Christian position is that we accept and believe this testimony, that these things here reported have happened. We base it solidly upon the authority and the testimony of these men of God.

Now the argument does not stop at that. You can test the witness of these men. There are many supporting arguments, but, basically, it is what they say, and we are shut down to their witness. Take out the apostolic testimony and what do we know about Jesus Christ apart from it? It is there that the whole arrogance of sin is manifested. It is in the higher critical movement of the nineteenth century when men sat down in their studies to reconstruct their 'Jesus of History'. But what do they know about that apart from these documents? For our knowledge we come back to these; it is a testimony that holds together this complete whole view; take parts out of it and it becomes lop-sided. It either has to be taken as it is or rejected *in toto*.

First and foremost, therefore, there is the report and then my experience as the result of believing the report. Thank God, it is supported by experience, but experience can never do anything beyond supporting it. Do not base your life upon your experience, because you may be sadly disillusioned. Base it upon these facts and then your experience will be a true one.

Then we move on from that to the next matter, which is central. The gospel, I repeat, is a declaration, a showing, and it comes to us on the authority of the Apostles; so what is its message? And the answer that we find here is that the essence of its message is Jesus Christ. 'That is our report,' says John. 'Here we are in this difficult and trying world, so what have I to say to you? Well,' he says, 'I have the most amazing and unbelievable thing that a man can ever say and I have nothing else to add. It is this: the Word of life was made flesh and dwelt amongst us.'

'(We beheld His glory, the glory as of the only begotten of the Father,) full of grace and truth' (Jn 1:14). That is how he puts it in his Gospel, and he really says much the same thing here. This is how he puts it: 'That which was from the beginning'– 'In the beginning,' he says in John 1:1; it is the same thing—before time, away in eternity. There was no beginning; it is endless, it is eternal; that is his way of describing it. We are in time, we are limited in our conception, and we cannot understand eternity; so, because of the limitation of time, when we try to describe eternity we have to say, 'in the beginning'; by which we mean there was no beginning. It sounds paradoxical, but there is no better expression of it. 'That which was from the beginning'; that which has always been, which has come out from that endless eternity. That is the first thing and he also puts it another way: 'In the beginning was the Word, and the Word was with God' (Jn 1:1)—with the Father in eternity.

Then the next thing is that this was *manifested*. We have heard, says John, but also 'we have seen', 'we have handled'. Now these terms are all of the greatest interest, there is a kind of order in them. The first thing it says is that we have heard, then we have seen. We may hear a voice and we think we know whose its is, but we cannot be sure until we have seen.

However, it does not stop at that. John seems to repeat himself, but he does not really. He adds to it–'that which we have seen with our eyes, *which we have looked upon*'. You see, there is a difference between seeing and looking upon. Seeing is the result of something confronting us; we are not looking for it, examining carefully. We may be walking along a street and we suddenly become aware of something—we have 'seen' it. 'Ah,' says John, 'we have not only seen. We have looked upon, we have investigated, and not with a mere cursory glance. We watched and we beheld. We looked at him, we sat in amazement, and we really have examined. And, further, our hands have handled of the Word of life.' It is as if John were saying here, 'I once reclined upon His bosom at a feast we all had together before He left us; I handled Him, I touched Him.' Remember the point which we made about Gnosticism and see how John deals with it here. Christ was not a phantom. No, 'the Word was made flesh', 'we have seen, we have beheld, we have examined, we have handled it'. He underlines the reality of it all. It was not a phantom body. The incarnation is a fact—'from the beginning' but here in time.

But he also reminds us that Christ even rose from the dead in that self-same body. Surely that can be the only adequate explanation of these words here—'and our hands have handled of the Word of life.' You remember the other Gnostic idea: how some of them said that the eternal Christ had entered into the man Jesus at His baptism and left Him on the cross so it was only the man Jesus who died. 'No,' says John, 'the one who died was God and man and He rose from the grave in the same body; and we know that because we have handled . . .' You see the difference? We read in Luke's Gospel that our Lord appeared in the body after His resurrection. The disciples would not believe it—they thought He was a spirit—but He said, 'Behold my hands and my feet.' 'We have handled Him,' says John. 'Handle me,' said the risen Christ, 'and see; for a spirit hath not flesh and bones, as ye see me have' (Lk 24:39). He rose in the body; He was the Son of God, and it was the Son of God who rose again. He is God-man, the one person with the two natures.

That, no doubt, was what was in John's mind as he wrote that prologue to his Gospel: 'And we beheld his glory . . .' (Jn 1:14). I think he is referring to the Mount of Transfiguration for one thing. When Jesus was transfigured He appeared in a transcendent glory—'We saw it,' says John, 'and we have never forgotten it. And then there was the glory of the resurrection; we beheld it, looked upon it.'

That is the whole message of the gospel. He leaves eternity and comes into time, and He goes back into eternity. 'The message we have proclaimed to you,' says John in effect, 'is this in its essence:

that on the face of this very earth on which you are still living, with its problems and trials and tribulations, on this very earth the Son of God Himself has come. We have had the amazing privilege of seeing Him, of hearing Him, of examining Him and touching Him and listening to Him—God, the Son of God, was amongst us and it has changed everything. I want to tell you about it so that you may share with us, and our sharing is with the Father and His Son Jesus Christ.'

But let me show you also that John's emphasis here is somewhat different from that of his Gospel. In the Gospel, John's main concern was to prove and to show that Jesus of Nazareth is none other than the eternal Son of God—that is its great message. But that is not the main message in this epistle. It is there, which is why he starts with it, as he must, but here he is concerned to show what that means and what it means *to us*. So he puts it like this. He refers to Him as the 'Word of life'; the Word that not only shows life, but gives life. So his emphasis is like this: 'The Son of God,' he says, 'came on earth not only to show us and to reveal to us the life of the Father. He did do that, for in Him the life of God has been manifested and unveiled. We have seen God in the flesh; as He said Himself, "He that hath seen me hath seen the Father" (Jn 14:9)—look at Him and you see that Father, the divine life.

'But it does not stop at that,' says John. 'Thank God, He came not only to reveal that eternal life, but also to impart it, to give it, to make it possible for us.' The Son of God, as John Calvin put it once and for all, became the Son of man that the sinful sons of men might become the sons of God. He is the Word of Life. The life was manifested, we have seen it, John declares, and that is the great theme of the epistle. That is why he starts with the phrase that has often confused people—'That which was from the beginning'—he is referring to Jesus Christ.

In other words, he already has the great idea in his mind, the great idea that there is possible to us in this world of time a divine life, a divine order of life; we can, indeed, possess the life of God. 'That life,' says John, 'was in Christ to all eternity; He has come and revealed and manifested it.' And he is thinking about the life that you and I can receive, and that is his great and glorious message—

that you and I can become partakers of the divine nature and sharers of the divine life itself.

That, then, is the message of the Christian Church to this weary, tired and frustrated world. What is going to happen to it? Let the governments do their utmost—it is their business to do so, for God has ordered governments to keep law and order. So let the government produce order and let all Christian people do their best to be law-abiding citizens in this and every other land. But the message of the gospel is to tell us that though all and every attempt at human order may fail, if we believe on the Lord Jesus Christ we have become children of God and citizens of the kingdom of heaven, a kingdom that can never be shaken and that will last world without end.

5

Christian Experience

That which we have seen and heard declare we unto you, that ye also may have fellowship with us: and truly our fellowship is with the Father, and with his Son Jesus Christ.

1 JOHN 1:3

Here in this verse the Apostle makes the first explicit statement in the letter of what is one of his main objects in writing to these people. The fundamental reason, as we have seen, is: 'these things write we unto you that your joy may be full', and his case is that one of the first essentials and absolute essentials to true joy, in a world such as this, is that we should realise this wondrous, glorious possibility that lies open to us of fellowship, of communion, of sharing in the life of God.

So now, we come to what is one of the big, basic themes of the entire epistle. It is, of course, a great theme also of the whole of the New Testament; indeed it is one of the profoundest, and at the same time perhaps one of the most difficult of all the New Testament themes. It is the central core of the New Testament message; but for that reason, and because there is an adversary of our souls, it is one that, right up to our own day, has frequently been misunderstood and misinterpreted.

There have been, I suppose, more heresies and more errors with regard to this epistle, and as to what is meant by this fellowship, than perhaps with any other matter. Therefore we approach it, not with trepidation, nor with fear, but with carefulness, realising that there are pitfalls and dangers all around us. And yet, it is of all truths, perhaps, the most glorious and the most wonderful. All other doctrines, in a sense, lead to this; all other aspects of truth are destined ultimately to bring us face to face with that which we find here.

Now it is a very large subject, and obviously one which no one should even attempt to deal with hurriedly. It has various aspects and first of all I want to deal in particular with one of them. In doing this, I take my line of approach from what is said by the Apostle himself. Here he is, an old man, at the end of his life, and he is writing to these Christians. Some were old, some were middle-aged, and some were young, and you will find that in the next chapter he divides them up like that and makes a special appeal to them— 'fathers', 'young men', 'little children', and so on. He knows about their world; he is in it too, and he is a man who himself has suffered a great deal. He knows what they are enduring; he knows the fight in which they are engaged and he wants to help and encourage them—that is his reason for writing. So he immediately begins to tell them that he has an astounding and extraordinary, almost incredible message to give them.

As we have seen, he has declared to them his certainty about the incarnation and the resurrection. And now the next thing he proceeds to deal with and to emphasise is the fact that the whole point and purpose of the coming of the Son of God into the world in that way was to give to those who believe on Him this amazing gift of eternal life. Now 'eternal' not only concerns duration; it does mean that, but it means something else also. Eternal life means life of a certain quality. Life in this world is not only a temporary limited life; actually, as far as death is concerned, it is always, in a sense, a living death. Life outside God is not life, it is existence, for there is a difference between the two.

You remember how our Lord put it in that great high priestly prayer recorded in John 17:3: 'And this is life eternal, that they might know thee the only true God, and Jesus Christ, whom thou hast sent.' Eternal life always carried that suggestion. Apart from God, life, as we call it, is really death; we are all born in trespasses and sin. We exist, yes, but we are spiritually dead. But eternal life is the true life. It is an endless life, but it is, in addition, a life with a different quality; it is really life in a sense that nothing else is. And that, John tells these people, is what has been made possible to all who believe on the Lord Jesus Christ.

But I am particularly anxious, at this point, to emphasise that in the following way. John, you notice, puts it like this: 'That which we have seen and heard declare we unto you, *that ye also may have fellowship with us.*' Now we shall have to go on to consider his further statement that 'our fellowship truly is with the Father and with his Son Jesus Christ', but the first thing that John says, in effect, is, 'I am writing to you in order that you may share the experience that we have had.' He says that he and the other Apostles, as a result of what they have seen and heard and felt and touched and handled, as the result of their belief on the Lord Jesus Christ, have experienced something, and he wants these people now to share in that experience to the full.

Let us, therefore, consider this Christian experience in a preliminary manner. We must examine it in general before we come to see in detail exactly what it is. And perhaps the best way of doing this is to put it in the form of a number of propositions which seem to me to be quite inevitable. What the Apostle says here about himself and his fellow Apostles is, according to the New Testament, something that should be true of every Christian, and these are the things he says.

The first is that Christians are people who know what they have. The Christian experience, in other words, is a definite and a certain experience—'that which we have seen and heard declare we unto you, that ye also may have fellowship with us.' Now if people do not know what they have, how can they wish for others to share it with them? So that is the starting point—that the Christian experience is not a vague one; it is not indefinite or uncertain. Rather, it is a well defined experience, and true Christians know what they have; they are aware of what they possess; they are in no uncertainty themselves as to what has happened to them and as to their personal position. 'We write these things to you,' says John, 'that your joy may be full', and that you may share what we have got, and you cannot invite someone to share something with you unless you know exactly what you are asking him to share.

This is quite elementary and surely needs no demonstration, and yet I am emphasising it and starting with it because of course we are all aware that not only is this not taken for granted, as it should be by Christian people, but that also it has often been a doctrine that has been much questioned and queried.

We are dealing with what may be called the great New Testament doctrine of the assurance of salvation, and it has been one which has been subjected to considerable criticism. People have regarded it as presumption. They have said that this is something which is impossible, and that no one should be able to claim such a thing. How often have we heard about 'the quest for truth' and all the sentimentality that accompanies such talk. People speak of the thrill and the excitement in this quest and Christians are pictured as mountaineers seeking for some great height.

But there is nothing like that in the New Testament—'these things *declare* we unto you.' 'I am writing,' says John, in effect, 'not because I am looking or seeking for truth, but because I have found it. I would not be writing if I had not found it, and I want you to experience the same thing.' He is not seeking or striving, nor is he just hoping. The position of John when he wrote this letter was not: 'Here I am an old man. I am drawing to the end and I had hoped that sometime this side of death the heavens would be rent and I would suddenly have a clear understanding of these things. Perhaps, however, I may have to wait until I have gone through death and awakened in another world; then I shall begin to see and understand these things.'

Not at all! Here is a man who tells us that he *knows*; and it is because he knows and because of what he has experienced that he is writing. Christians are not men and women who are hoping for salvation, but those who have experienced it. They have it; there is no uncertainty; they 'know in whom [they] have believed' (2 Tim 1:12); and it is because John has possessed this that he writes about it.

So this, surely, is something which is quite fundamental and basic. I verily believe that half our troubles in the Christian life, and indeed most of our unhappiness and our failure to share in the experience of these first Christians, is due to this initial prejudice which we seem to have as the result of sin, and by nature, against the doctrine of assurance of salvation. Yet I suggest to you that you cannot read the New Testament without seeing clearly that all these men and women, the ones who wrote and the ones to whom the letters are addressed, are those who, according to this teaching, know for certain. There can be no true joy of salvation while there is a vagueness or an uncertainty or a lack of assurance with respect to what we have.

Now I am not saying that we cannot be Christians without this assurance of salvation, but I am saying that if we want to have the New Testament experience, if we want to be like the saints of the centuries, then we must have it. Thank God, we, by His infinite grace, are in Christ even if we may remain ignorant about these things. Assurance is not essential to salvation, but it is essential to the joy of salvation.

We can support this by making a second statement. Christians are not only people who know what they have; they are also anxious for all others to have and possess it. And that, of course, is the final proof of their certainty of that which they have: 'That which we have seen and heard declare we unto you'—why?— *'that ye also may have fellowship with us.'* John was anxious that these people should have exactly the same thing he and the other Apostles possessed. That is first and foremost the proof of his certainty as to what he has got. But he also indicates that those who have truly had this Christian experience and who have realised it fully, long for all others to have the same thing.

We are dealing with profound matters here, matters which will test us at the very depths of our whole position as Christian people. Surely this needs no argument or demonstration. Those who have become conscious of the fact that they are sharing the life of God—those who know what it is to rejoice and what it is to be emancipated from certain besetting sins which hitherto always got them down—those who can see through life and who have overcome the world—those to whom death has lost its sting and who know at times what it is even to long to go beyond the veil and to be with

Christ in glory—men and women who have had some experience of these things of necessity want others to feel the same.

That is why you find so constantly in the pages of the New Testament that this is one of the tests of the Christian. Am I anxious that others should have what I possess? Am I sorry for men and women in the world around and about me who lack this experience? Some of Paul's great verses express this: he says, 'I am debtor both to the Greeks, and to the Barbarians; both to the wise, and to the unwise. So, as much as in me is, I am ready to preach the gospel to you that are at Rome also' (Rom 1:14-15). He says again, 'For the love of Christ constraineth us' (2 Cor 5:14), and 'Woe is unto me, if I preach not the gospel!' (1 Cor 9:16). He said these things because of the transcendent nature of the experience, and he has a sense of pity and compassion for all who lack it. Christians, in other words, are like their Lord and Master. We are told of our Lord that He looked upon the people and saw them as sheep without a shepherd, and He had compassion upon them. And that is the characteristic of these New Testament disciples. They are sorry for those who are walking in darkness.

Christian people, here is the question that comes to us at a time like this. What is our attitude towards men and women around and about us who are not concerned about these things, who are heedless about them? Have we a sense of compassion for them? Do we know what it is to feel that we will do anything we can in order to make them have what we have got? That is the Christian position, so that, by nature, all who are in Christ have this missionary spirit, this desire for others to have and to share with them the thing that they themselves possess; it is inevitable by definition.

The third principle is perhaps still more important. Christian experience in the life of all believers is always essentially the same experience. I regard this as vital for this reason: that it is because of this that we are able to test our Christian experience, and there are those who would say that the whole purpose of this first epistle of John is to do this. A famous commentary on this epistle written by Robert Law bears that very name—*The Tests of Life*.

Now this is a very important subject. Let us look at it like this. The Apostle tells these people that he longs for them to share with him and the other Apostles the experience that they have. In other words we can lay down this fundamental rule: no one can be a Christian without experiencing what the first Apostles experienced. 'We,' says John in effect, 'were eyewitnesses; we saw, we handled, we touched, we heard. He spoke to us, He breathed the Holy Ghost upon us and we received this blessing from Him. Now,' he says, 'we want you all to come and share this joy and experience with us'; it is the same experience.

This is something, I think, which can be established as a fact of history. It has often been said, and rightly so, that every true revival of religion is a return to the first-century religion; every re-awakening that takes place is just a return on the part of the Church to that which is described in the book of the Acts of the Apostles. That is profoundly true, and if you read the histories of revivals, you will find that in a most extraordinary manner. Revivals repeat one another; there is nothing that is more fascinating than to take the outstanding characteristics of the revivals of the different centuries, and you will find that they are always the same. The same kind of phenomena, the same kind of experience, the same kind of results. It is always a return to that primitive experience, the very thing that John tells us here, sharing, participating in his experience and that of the other Apostles.

We can look at it in another way. Take the biographies or auto-biographies of some of the most outstanding saints that the Church has ever known; and again you will find absolutely the same thing, this peculiar sameness, this common element. It is one of the most thrilling things, when reading church history, to observe this constantly being repeated. Let me give one example. When Martin Luther, under the influence of the Spirit of God, was brought to his great experience of salvation, there was nothing that so amazed and thrilled him, as he worked out his Christian doctrine, as the fact that he had been rediscovering for himself everything that St. Augustine had said in his writings; while Augustine found that he had been reiterating the things that had been written by the Apostle Paul! And so it has been throughout the centuries.

Let us emphasise this by putting it negatively: the Christian experience does not vary with the individual. Let me be careful to safeguard that by indicating clearly what I mean. It is not that the means of entry into the experience is always exactly the same. Someone sees God in a service; others tell us that in reading their Bible they found Him. That does not matter; I am speaking of the experience itself, not of the way in which we enter it, and I am at pains to emphasise this because it is our final answer to the attack which is made upon the Christian position by psychology.

'Ah,' says the psychologist, 'these things are a matter of temperament, and people differ from case to case in their temperament and psychology.' But the glorious thing about the Christian experience is that whatever their natural psychology, whatever their natural temperament, all Christians experience essentially the same experience as one another. There are variations even amongst the Apostles; some are impulsive, some are logical, some are morbid, and yet the glory is that they all have the same central experience. The Christian faith can make a morbid man rejoice, it can take a natural pessimist and make him rejoice in tribulation. Regardless of individuality or temperament, all can know this same experience; it does not vary from individual to individual, nor does it vary from century to century.

Our central sin in this twentieth century is, of course, to believe that there have never been people like ourselves. We are essentially people of culture and development and how often do modern men and women say, 'The great people in the past used to believe and experience certain things, but we, with our different background and setting, must not go back to those things because we must have something peculiar to this century.' But this experience is quite independent of centuries; it is the eternal entering into time. Examine these Christians in every century and you will find that the experience is the same, and the greatest need of the twentieth century is to have the experience of the first century.

Why do we stress this? Firstly, because this experience is not primarily something subjective; it is, rather, the result of something which is based upon the belief of an objective truth. Merely subjective experience varies from individual to individual, from time to time and from situation to situation; but here is an experience which is common to all Christians because it is based upon an objective truth. 'That which was from the beginning which we have heard, which we have seen with our eyes, which we have looked upon and which our hands have handled of the Word of life.'

John does not say, 'I have had a marvellous experience and so have the other Apostles.' No, rather John says, 'We have seen, we have heard'—it is all something that comes out of Christ. It is based on objective truth; it is a response and a reaction to that, and because it is not primarily subjective, you have this element of sameness.

Secondly, Christian experience is not only based on objective truth, it is always based upon the *same* truth—it is always based upon Christ, it always emanates from Him. You see, John puts Christ at the beginning; everything is related to Him, and because it is always an experience which results from the same truth, it must be essentially the same experience; the same cause leads to the same effect.

To put it another way, the Christian experience is based upon the receiving of eternal life; God is the giver of eternal life in Christ—the same giver, the same gift and, therefore, the same experience. Now if our Christian experience were based upon our understanding or upon our activities or our efforts, obviously it would differ from case to case. The intelligent and the unintelligent person would not have the same experience; but the glory of this position is that we all receive salvation as a free gift from God. It is the same gift of life, and because it is the same giver and the same gift it must be essentially the same experience.

So if all that is true—and indeed it is profoundly so—then the experience which we have is one which can be tested and examined. Now we shall have to revert to this many times in working through the epistle. John is concerned about testing experience. You will find that later on where he exhorts these people to prove the spirits and to test them. This is because, as we have seen, there were Gnostics in the early Church and a further part of their teaching was this. They said, 'We have had an experience, with marvellous visions, but you must not question or examine it.' They regarded it as a secret which must be neither questioned nor examined. There are still people like that. They say, 'I am not interested in your doctrine or in your theology and dogma. I have experienced something; something has happened to me, so I must not be examined, because it is very secret.'

But that, according to the New Testament, is the height of error, because this experience which the Christian has is, as we have just seen, always a repetition of the apostolic experience, because it is always based upon the same truth and is the result of the same gift from the same giver. It is an experience that we can test, we can ask it questions, and that is the only way to safeguard ourselves against the false mysticisms and the false teaching which would masquerade as true Christian teaching, but in reality is nothing but something psychological or perhaps even psychic.

And this is as relevant in this modern world as it was in the first century. There are teachers today claiming to know about a 'higher Christian life' for those of us who are but ordinary, average church members. They would have us listen to their teaching, and they tell us that their teaching is something that has come to them because of some wonderful experience they have had. They say no one else can understand it, but they have experienced it. Now this is not what the Apostle is emphasising. His experience is one that is based upon objective truth and teaching. It can be tested, it can be examined; indeed I go further and say it *must* be tested, it must be examined, for there are seducers, there are anti-Christs and there are evil spirits. So test the spirits, prove the spirits, 'prove all things; hold fast that which is good' (1 Thess 5:21). So that far from resenting an examination of our experiences, if we are truly Christian, we will welcome an examination and we will rejoice in it.

And the test of course is none other than that of the Word itself. Here is the test—the apostolic record, the apostolic witness, the apostolic testimony. If my experience does not tally with the New Testament, it is not the Christian experience. It may be wonderful, it may be thrilling, I may have seen visions. But, I say, it matters not at all; if my experience does not tally with this, it is not the Christian experience. How vital it is, therefore, to grasp this central truth.

Lastly, the experience is one which is possible for all. 'That which we have seen and heard declare we unto you, that ye also may have fellowship with us.' Thank God this is an experience, not only for the Apostles because they were with Christ, it is equally possible for us. We must all grasp this. Have we not often felt something like this: 'If only I could have been there when Christ was here in the flesh; if only I could have looked into His eyes and seen and heard Him, why, it would be so much easier to believe!'

But that is an utter fallacy–'What we have seen we declare unto you,' says John. 'The experience is as possible for you as it is for us. You have never seen Him; we saw Him, but you can have the same experience.' So it was not only for the first Apostles but for us also. Never discount the writings of Paul, John and Peter therefore, and say, 'That was all right for them, but it is not meant for me.' It is meant for all; it is meant for us.

Furthermore, it is not only for people with a certain temperament, for those who are said to have a 'religious temperament'; it is for everyone because the sameness of the experience, as we have seen, is due to the sameness of the Giver and of the gift. It is possible to all of us, because it is not in any way based upon us but entirely upon Him and upon His grace and upon His desire and His readiness to give.

Finally, what is the experience? The experience is fellowship 'with the Father and with His Son, Jesus Christ'. To know God! We saw at the beginning that the Christian knows what he has got. So that is the question. Do you know God? And has this knowledge of God given you something in your life that makes you long for others to share it with you? Do you understand the experience outlined in the New Testament? Do you say, as you read it, 'Yes, I know that; I know what it means when he talks of a "new man" and an "old man". I know what he means when he talks about being lifted up above myself and having a knowledge of things unseen, and I know the influence of the Holy Spirit.' This is an experience which is concrete and which can be tested and examined, and it makes us participants of that of which these Apostles wrote so gloriously in the New Testament epistles.

May God give us grace to examine ourselves in the light of these truths. This wonderful experience never varies; it is always essentially the same. Let us make certain that we are sharers in the apostolic experience of a knowledge of God and of receiving eternal life through Him.

6

All Because of Christ

That which we have seen and heard declare we unto you, that ye also may have fellowship with us: and truly our fellowship is with the Father, and with his Son Jesus Christ.

1 JOHN 1:3

A s men and women look at the world in which they live, with its wars, its vicissitudes, its false hopes and all its suffering, those who are not content with observing these things merely on a superficial level, and who have any true interest or concern, are bound to ask the questions: What is the trouble; what is the difficulty; why is the world as it is?

And it is just at that point, of course, that as Christian people we have something very special and vital to say; it is just there in a sense that the Christian gospel comes in. And surely, if we as individual Christians are called upon to do one thing more than any other at the present time, it is to proclaim the word of the gospel; it is to speak the word of God in that situation and just in that very connection. That is the point where the world comes to an end in its thinking; it is baffled, it does not understand; all its prophecies have been falsified, all its confident hopes have been dashed to the ground, and the world is thus undoubtedly bewildered.

And if it is just there that we as Christians come in, it is also especially at that point that the message of this first epistle of John comes in with its specific message. As we have already seen,

67

Christians are not surprised at the state of the world; indeed it is a strange confirmation of their attitude towards life and towards the whole history of the world; for they start, as we have been reminded in our study of this epistle, with the fundamental postulate that 'the whole world lieth in the wicked one'.

Here again, you see, we have one of those illustrations of what the Psalmist meant when he said so perfectly, 'Surely, the wrath of man shall praise thee' (Ps 76:10); and the wrath of man praises God, amongst other things, in that particular way; the very wrath of man that produces a world such as this is a world which is proving the contention of the Bible, that the world is in the power of 'the god of this world', 'the prince of the power of the air'—these various titles which are ascribed to that malign evil power that has set itself in rebellion against God.

Christians, therefore, are not surprised. They understand; they know that there is a radical evil in life as the result of sin and the Fall, and that while that remains there can be nothing in the world except what we have experienced. So they are saved at once from becoming excited about the various false hopes, and they are also saved from the cynicism of this period. This twentieth century is a great reaction from the nineteenth, which was so full of its confident hopes and expectations. Now we are experiencing the reaction, and the average person has become cynical and unconcerned. The philosophy of today is, 'What is the use of anything, the whole world seems to be mad, therefore let us make the best of a bad job.'

Now the Christian is saved from all that immediately, but, thank God, it does not stop at that, it is not merely something negative. The gospel of Jesus Christ gives us a satisfactory explanation of why the world is as it is, and it puts it like this in its essence. It says that all the trouble is due to man's rebellion against God, and to nothing else. We are delivered from the waste of time of trying to analyse political theories. Wars cannot be explained in those terms. You cannot explain wars merely in terms of men like Hitler and others, or of the aggression of one particular nation.[1] Political, economic and social ideas and theories are finally quite inadequate, and with our Christian insight we see things; we know that the explanation is something which is very much deeper. These other things are but the manifestations, for the radical cause of the trouble is that men and women, in their folly, are in a state of rebellion against God.

This is the very essence of the biblical message, that man and woman, placed by God in a state of paradise and perfection, felt that even paradise was an insult to them because there was subjection to God. It was that original act of rebellion that led to all their other troubles—that is the story of the Bible. This initial act of rebellion produced fear in them; once they knew they had done something they should not have done, that caused them to look at each other with jealously and envy. Then the children came, and they were envious and jealous and so on; sorrow came after sorrow. And it can all be traced back to the fact that men and women were really meant to live a life in communion with God, and that happiness, in a full and final sense, is only really possible when they obey the law of their own being; and that as long as they refuse to do that, they can experience nothing but turmoil and unhappiness and wretchedness.

This, says the Bible, is the state of the world away from God. It rebels against God and therefore produces its own miseries. It does not argue about that, it just tells us, and the whole state of the world is just a proof of that. It is no use, says the Bible; you can do what you like, you can organise and scheme as much as you like, but while men and women are in a wrong relationship to God, they can never be better. As Augustine put it: 'Thou hast made us for Thyself, and our souls are restless until they find their rest in Thee.' That is the trouble with the individual and with groups and with society and with nations and thus, ultimately, with the whole world. So, because of sin we are in a world like this, and the world is like this because of sin.

So the questions arise: Is there any hope for us? Can anything be done for us? What is the message of the Christian Church to a world like ours, what has she to say? Here, of course, we come again to the vital question especially for the Church and for the preachers of the Church. Is it the business of Church to try to analyse the situation by putting forward proposals? Is she to throw out suggestions to the statesmen and 'the powers that be' as to how they should order the society of the world? Is she to make application for the adoption of certain Christian principles?

Now, as I understand the Bible, all that is a pure waste of time! Again I suggest that history substantiates and proves my position. The Church has been doing that for many years; she has turned to what has been called the 'social gospel', and we have constantly heard about 'the social application of the gospel'. General statements are made about life; addresses are delivered by archbishops and they are all always recorded in the Press; but still the situation continues. And according to the Bible it must continue. What right have we to expect Christian behaviour from a world that does not believe in Christ? Why should the world apply Christian principles? Does it believe in Christ, does it acknowledge Him to be who He is? Does it accept Him as Saviour?

Indeed, I do not hesitate to say that according to the New Testament it is rank heresy to recommend Christian behaviour to people who are not Christian. They are incapable of it! Before people can live the Christian life they must be made a new creation; if they cannot keep the moral law and the Ten Commandments, the ancient law given to the Children of Israel, how can they live according to the Sermon on the Mount? How can they follow Christ? It is ridiculous! That is not our message; that is not what the Church must say.

No, the Church must address individuals, and her address to them is something like this. It is not for the Church to prophesy what the future is going to be because we do not know. But we do know that whatever the Church may say in the form of these vague generalities it will make no difference. The New Testament, however, comes to me as an individual and says, 'That is the story of the world you are in. If you expect it suddenly to turn over a new leaf, to become perfect and to live the Sermon on the Mount, then your theology is all wrong. In a world that lies under the power of the evil one you can expect nothing but evil and wars.'

'Oh, how depressing,' says someone. But facts can be depressing; and whether they are depressing or not, the business of the wise man and woman is to face those facts. The New Testament is realistic, and it does not hold out hope of a glorious future in terms of the human race and its actions. Rather, it paints a very solemn picture. But it does not stop at that. It comes to us and says, 'In such a world what is possible for you? What is there that you can hold on to? Is there a message that comes to you in such a world, which is going to transform everything for you?' And the answer is, 'Here is the message', and that is the essence of what John immediately plunges into at the commencement of his epistle.

The cause of our troubles, as we have seen, is that we have rebelled against God. We are in the wrong relationship to Him, and we have lost the fact of God. We no longer know Him; we are out of communion and fellowship with Him. That is our trouble, and we have been so made by God that there is something within us that can never be at rest until we get back to that. There is always something lacking until we know God. The supreme need of the world, and of people as individuals, is a knowledge of God, fellowship with Him and communion with Him, and that, says the Bible, is the central need. We can never be in communion with others until we are in true communion with God. The Apostle Paul says this in Ephesians 2. 'You have been made one,' says Paul, referring to Jews and Gentiles, 'because you have both been put right with God in Christ. The middle wall of partition has been broken down' (Eph 2:11-22).

So man rises against man and nation against nation because each one does not recognise God, and the only way to reconcile man with man is that both should be reconciled to God. The supreme need for every one of us is to know God, to return to that condition of fellowship and communion, to know that centrally I am right with Him. 'That,' says John in effect, 'is the message I have to give you, and it is a glorious one'; that is why he pours it forth without any introduction whatever. 'Because of what has happened,' says John, 'because of the coming of Christ who is the Son of God and the substance of the eternal substance; because of Him and His coming and of what He has done, it is possible for you to be in fellowship with God'–'our fellowship is with the Father and with his Son, Jesus Christ.'

Now there are those who would say that this verse should be read like this–'our fellowship is with the Father, by means of and through His Son, Jesus Christ.' I believe that both ways of looking at the verse are correct; we have fellowship with the Father and with the Son separately, and undoubtedly the great message of the New Testament is that fellowship with the Father is now possible in and through the Son, our Lord and Saviour Jesus Christ. So the question I want to consider now is: how has Jesus Christ made this fellowship with the Father possible? What has He done? In other words, we look back at Him. 'We declare,' says John; 'we remember Him.' Every act of preaching is in a sense nothing but a reminder of Jesus Christ and what He came to do. That is the meaning of the Communion Service also, with the bread and the wine; He told his disciples to remember Him. The whole witness of the Church is a witness to Him, and our business in this world is to tell men and women to remember Jesus Christ, to turn back and look at Him. So thus you see we are raised from the human to the divine level.

What, then, is the basic element of this fellowship? How can we be reconciled to God and have communion with Him; how can we have fellowship with others? In what sense is any sort of peace possible amongst people in a world like this? Well, according to John, it is all something that is based upon our Lord Jesus Christ. It is He who has made it possible.

There are certain things that are essential before you can have fellowship. Firstly, there must be no obstacles or barriers, for if there is anything like that between two persons, there is no true fellowship. If there is suspicion or distrust, if there is a question or query as to motive or whether we can trust one another; if there is a grudge, if there is something that has been done and has wounded or hurt the other, fellowship is immediately impossible. Fellowship demands and insists upon the removal of every barrier and every obstacle, anything that is doubtful or uncertain or that can come between. That is essential before there can be true fellowship, and it is in the light of that that we begin to understand the work of our Lord and Saviour Jesus Christ.

Why is man outside the life of God? The answer of the Bible is that there is a mighty obstacle between God and man, and that obstacle is called sin. Sin came in between man and God. It can be regarded as a terrible cloud of blackness and darkness. Before the cloud man looked into the face of God, but the cloud of sin came in and there it remains. This must be regarded from two aspects, of course. Sin keeps a barrier between God and us, for God is holy and God cannot look lightly upon sin. God had warned man that if he sinned he should die. He told him that if he went where he had been forbidden, he would merit punishment, and the punishment would be nothing but death, spiritual death as well as physical. And spiritual death means the loss of the face of God and communion with Him. Man sinned, and the wrath of God came in. So there is a barrier between God and man.

And that, on the other side, brings in a barrier between man and God in this way, that man with his guilty conscience feels that God is unfair. A disobedient child always begins to dislike the parent. Guilt always has that effect; it always attempts to excuse itself and to put the blame on to the other person. So men and women, in sin and in a state of guilt, begin to have unfair and unworthy thoughts against God. We say that there should not be such laws and, further, that there should never be punishment, even if there are such laws. So we argue and put up this barrier between ourselves and God. We cannot see Him because our guilty thoughts have come between us and Him. There is no friendship and trust; there is an obstacle between God and man in that way. 'The thrilling thing I have to tell you,' says John to these people, 'is that as the result of the coming into this world of Jesus of Nazareth, who is the only begotten Son of God, and as the result of what He has done, I declare unto you that we have fellowship with the Father; the very thing we lost has been restored!'

How then has it been restored? Firstly, He has dealt with the obstacle and barrier of sin—that is why we 'declare the Lord's death till He come'; that is why the Cross must ever be at the centre of Christian preaching. I cannot face God apart from the Cross. That is why the 'mystic' way apart from the Cross is a delusion and a snare; that is why also good works and our good resolutions are something again which lead us astray—the barrier has to be dealt with. The justice and righteousness of the holy God demand that sin should be punished; God cannot say a thing and then withdraw it; God cannot speak and then deny it, and He has said that sinners must be punished. God's law and God's word remain absolute—they cannot be avoided. But Christ has come into the world, and by His infinite act of surrender and consecration He has offered Himself to the Father and called upon the Father to lay upon His holy body, His holy life, the sins of the world. As John says in the next chapter, 'He is the propitiation for our sins: and not for ours only, but also for the sins of the whole world' (1 Jn 2:2). 'The Lord hath laid on him the iniquity of us all' (Is 53:6).

You may not understand it, no one can, but it is the essence of the biblical message. God has done this astounding thing. He has punished your sin and mine there in Christ; our guilt has been removed; that obstacle, that barrier, has been taken away. God is satisfied; His wrath has been manifested upon the head of His only begotten innocent Son. The wrath of God because of sin is already revealed from heaven, says the Apostle Paul in writing to the Romans (Rom 1:18). God revealed His law, but this is the further revelation. It has now been revealed from heaven that God's wrath manifested itself to the full upon the head of Christ who died guilt-less and innocent for our sins; and thereby the obstacle has been removed.

In the same way, the moment we come to see that, the other aspect of the obstacle of sin is likewise dealt with; once we look at that cross and realise what happened there, our thoughts of God are entirely changed. We now see that God is a God of love, a God whose love is so amazing and divine that He even brings that to pass. Once we see God truly and Christ dying innocently on the cross for us, then at once we see that God is a God of love. So the obstacle has been taken from the other side also. In Christ there is no obstacle or barrier any longer; friendship has been restored; the enmity, as Paul puts it, has been removed and has been banished. That is the first essential.

The second is that before you can have true fellowship and communion there must be likeness, a fundamental sameness. This is another great theme of the Bible, and it is something we can also prove apart from the Bible. There are many people in this life whom we know, and in a sense we may like them; yet we feel we have no fellowship with them. There is something dissimilar; there is no identity of interests—we have not got this fundamental sameness. Before there can be true fellowship and communion there must be a likeness of nature. Paul has put this once and for ever in 2 Corinthians 6:14 when he says that there can be no fellowship between righteousness and unrighteousness, no communion between light and darkness. There are certain things in this world that cannot mix.

Now that applies to men and women in their relationship to God; before they can really know God and have fellowship and communion with Him they must be like Him. That is an astounding statement, yet it is the very language of the New Testament. The New Testament says that a man can never really know God until he has himself God's own nature, and that is precisely the claim of the Apostle John at this point. 'Our fellowship is with the Father, and with his Son Jesus Christ.' He is going to tell us how we have become 'sons of God', or, as Peter puts it, how we can become 'partakers of the divine nature' (2 Pet 1:4). It is Christ alone who makes that possible to us. John says that in Christ the eternal life was manifested (1 Jn 1:2), but He did not stop at that; He came to give us life. 'I am come,' He said, 'that they might have life, and that they might have it more abundantly' (Jn 10:10). 'Whoso eateth my flesh, and drinketh my blood,' He also said, 'hath eternal life' (Jn 6:54). 'I am that living bread which came down from heaven' (Jn 6:51); 'I am that living manna, that heavenly manna,' He said, 'you must eat and take of Me, and as you do so, you will receive life.'

So before we can have true fellowship with God we must have the nature of God; we must share His life, and in Christ that is made possible to us. We must not think of our Christian life merely as something which produces a doctrine of forgiveness—thank God we are forgiven, that must come first—but I cannot have fellowship with God before I am like Him, and in Christ I can receive a new life, a new nature. I can be born again, I can become 'a new man', and I can say with Paul, 'I live; yet not I, but Christ liveth in me' (Gal 2:20).

And, thirdly and lastly, we must love the same things. We must love one another, there must be no suspicion, there must be a complete understanding, there must be complete confidence and complete trust. Men and women apart from Christ may believe in God as a great power, or as Creator; they may believe in Him as the one who controls everything. We can have such philosophical notions and conceptions of God, but there is no fellowship without love, and it is only as we see Him in the Lord Jesus Christ that we truly come to love Him. 'God commendeth his love toward us in that while we were yet sinners, Christ died for us' (Rom 5:8), and no one ever has loved or can truly love Him until they see Him there in the person of His only begotten Son. God so loved, even unto death, that we guilty sinners might live.

There, says John, is the message I have for you in a world which is as it is because it is not in fellowship with God; a world which is unhappy and miserable and wretched and has its wars and all these things because it is out of communion with Him. The message is that even in a world like that, you can be restored to communion; the guilt of your sin has been removed, the image has been restored, and love for God has been created. And having this fellowship, we can experience what the Lord Jesus Christ Himself experienced. For we are told by the author of the epistle to the Hebrews that He, 'for the joy that was set before him endured the cross, despising the shame' (Heb 12:2). There may be troubles for us, in many ways the cross may come to us, but because of the communion He had with the Father, He was able even to go to the cruel, shameful death of the cross with joy in His heart and was able to despise the shame. And that is the offer of the gospel to all who believe on the Lord Jesus Christ. With this communion and fellowship we may smile, we may carry the cross, we may have perfect joy, though 'the whole world lieth in the wicked one'.

The ultimate question therefore is, do we have this joy of the Lord in spite of what may happen, in spite of grief and sorrow, in spite of uncertainty? Do we have this priceless possession which is offered us in the Lord Jesus Christ?

7

Knowing God

And truly our fellowship is with the
Father, and with his Son Jesus Christ.

1 JOHN 1:3

I am ready to admit that I approach a statement like this with fear
and trembling. It is one of those statements concerning which a
man feels that the injunction given to Moses of old at the burn-
ing bush is highly appropriate: 'Put off thy shoes from off thy feet;
for the place whereon thou standest is holy ground' (Ex 3:5). Here
we are given, without any hesitation, a description, the *summum
bonum*, of the Christian life; here, indeed, is the whole object, the
ultimate, the goal of all Christian experience and all Christian
endeavour. This, beyond any question, is the central message of the
Christian gospel and of the Christian faith.

The Apostle reminds us of that by this emphatic and vital word
truly—certainly, beyond a doubt. The word means that, but also
something else; it carries in it a suggestion of astonishment. There
is no doubt about it and yet the more we realise how true it is, the
more amazed we become. It is an amazement of incredulity, one
borne of a realisation of something which is a fact certainly, yet
astoundingly; to the natural man, incredible, but to the Christian
true, yet amazing. 'Truly, our fellowship is with the Father, and with
his Son Jesus Christ.' Here, let me repeat, is the very acme of

Christian experience and at the same time it is a goal; it is the whole object of Christian experience and of Christian faith and teaching.

Now I am tempted to put this matter in the form of a question. I wonder, as we examine ourselves and our experience, whether we all can say honestly that this is our central conception of the Christian life; whether this is our habitual way of thinking of it and of all that it means and all it represents. Surely as we read a statement like this we must be conscious of utter unworthiness and of failure. However far we may have advanced in the Christian life and experience, as we meet this statement, which John thus introduces without any preamble, do we not find that we are in danger of dwelling on the lower level and of failing to avail ourselves of that which is offered to us in this wondrous faith about which we are concerned?

Let me put it negatively like this: Christians are not simply people who are primarily concerned about the application of Christian principles and Christian teaching in all their relationships and departments of life. They are concerned about that, but that is not the thing that truly makes them Christian. How easy it is today to think of Christianity like that, and how many people do so.

Take a popular classification of a Christian and a non-Christian. Christian people are those who are concerned with the ethics and the teaching of the New Testament and who see the desperate need of applying them to the world today. Now I grant that that is part of the Christian life, but if our conception of it stops at that, we have not, in a sense, got anywhere near the definition given by the Apostle here. No, the Christian life is not essentially an application of teaching; it is a fellowship, a communion with God Himself and nothing less.

Or let me even put it like this: To be a Christian does not merely mean that you hold orthodox opinions on Christian teaching. I put it like that because I think that this is another important emphasis. Perhaps to some of us, and particularly perhaps to those of us who are more evangelical than others, this is the greatest danger of all. We recognise at once that there are certain people who call themselves Christian who hold views that are the antithesis of the Christian faith. There are people calling themselves Christian who deny the unique deity of Christ; to us they cannot be Christian. There are certain things, we say, which are absolutely essential and there can be no parleying or discussion about them. They are essential to the faith, there is an irreducible minimum, but there are people calling themselves Christian who deny some of these things, indeed perhaps all of them together. They may even hold office in the Christian Church and yet be uncertain about the person of the Lord, denying His miracles, denying the fact of His resurrection, denying the atoning value of His death.

Now to us that is quite clear. We see that someone like that, whatever he may call himself, cannot, according to the New Testament, be a Christian; there are certain things which Christians must believe; there are certain tenets to which they must subscribe; there are certain definitions which they must make their own and about which they say, 'I am certain.' We see that orthodoxy is essential, but my point here, and I am anxious to impress and stress this, is that to hold the right views, to subscribe to the right doctrine, even to be defenders of the right doctrine, does not of necessity make people Christians. No, while the Christian must hold right views and doctrines, that is not the essence of the Christian life and Christian position. Rather, it is to have fellowship with the Father and with His Son, Jesus Christ.

Let me even put it like this: To believe that your sins are forgiven by the death of Christ is not enough. Even to be sound on the whole doctrine of justification by faith only—the great watchword of the Protestant Reformation—that is not enough. That can be held as an intellectual opinion, and if people merely hold on to a number of orthodox opinions, they are not, I repeat, in the truly Christian position. The essence of the Christian position and of the Christian life is that we should be able to say, 'Truly my fellowship is with the Father, and with His Son Jesus Christ.'

That, therefore, is why we should always approach a statement like this with fear and trembling. There have been people in the Church, alas, many times in the past, who have fought for orthodoxy and who have been defenders of the faith and yet they have sometimes found themselves on their deathbeds coming to the realisation that they have never known God. They have only held opinions; they have only fought for certain articles of creed or faith. The things they fought for were right, but, alas, it is possible to stop at that negative position and to fail to realise that the whole object of all the things they claim to believe is to bring them to this central position.

This, let me emphasise again, is the essence, the *summum bonum*, of the Christian life; it is the theme, the objective of everything that has been done by the Lord Jesus Christ, who did not come to earth merely to give us an exalted teaching which we can apply to human relationships, though that is there and it follows; He did not come merely to save us from hell; He came to bring us into fellowship with the Father and with Himself.

This brings us directly face to face with the great question: what then does fellowship mean, what does it represent? 'If this is the great and central thing,' says someone, 'what do you mean by it?' Here again we come to a subject which has often been the cause of controversy. It has led to a good deal of dispute in the long history of the Christian Church, and especially, perhaps, when you come to consider the questions of how it is that one arrives in this state of fellowship and of how one can maintain it. We shall be considering these things later, but let us start now by looking directly at what is meant by this fellowship. We talk about the Christian as being one who has fellowship with God the Father and with God the Son, our Lord Jesus Christ, but what exactly does it mean?

Well, as one understands Scripture and its teaching, it seems to me there are two things at any rate which are true in this connection. The very word that the Apostle uses is an interesting one, this word *fellowship*. Those who are interested in words will know that this word has many different meanings. But a problem like this is not to be faced primarily theoretically. Dictionaries do not provide the answer. No, you have to take a word like this in the light of everything we are told about fellowship with God in the whole of the teaching of the Bible, and there are two things that stand out.

Firstly, to be in a state of fellowship means that we share in things; we are partakers, or, if you like, partners—that idea is there intrinsically in the word. That means something like this: The Christian is one who has become a sharer in the life of God. Now that is staggering and astounding language, but the Bible teaches us that; the New Testament offers us that, and nothing less than that.

Peter writes, 'Whereby are given unto us exceeding great and precious promises; that by these ye might be partakers of the divine nature, having escaped the corruption that is in the world through lust' (2 Pet 1:4). That is it, and there are many other similar statements. Indeed, the whole doctrine of regeneration and rebirth leads to this; born again, born from above, born of the Spirit–all carry exactly the same idea. This, then, is what John is so anxious to impress upon the minds of his readers; that Christians are not merely people who are a little bit better than they once were and who have just added certain things to their lives. Rather they are men and women who have received the divine life.

Now it is just there that the danger tends to come in. 'Is it something physical?' asks someone. 'Does it mean that a kind of divine essence comes into one?' There, you see, you have the whole host of teaching which has come in. The Roman Catholic Church would say that yes, this is something material, and that is why the sacraments are essential. In the application of the water which has been consecrated, the divine life is given to that child, and then as you partake of the mass and receive the host into your mouth, you are literally receiving something of the divine nature and essence. There we have to be careful, and it seems to me that the essence of wisdom at this point is that we should be careful not to go beyond the plain teaching of Scripture. How tempting it is to speculate, to philosophise, to try to work out in our own earthly categories that somehow or another some portion of the divine substance or essence enters into us.

There is only one safe thing to do and say and that is that we do not know; but in some amazing and astounding manner we know that we are partakers of the divine nature, that the being of God has somehow entered into us. I cannot tell you how, I cannot find it in the dissecting room. It is no use dissecting the body, you will not find it, any more than you will find the soul in dissecting the body, but it is here, it is in us, and we are aware of it. There is a being in us–'I live; yet not I, but Christ liveth in me' (Gal 2:20)– how, I do not know. We will understand in glory, but somehow we know now that we are sharers in the life of God, that we are partakers of the life and of the nature of God Himself, that we share it in communion, that we have partaken of it, we have participated in it, and we are in Him. We, somehow, are in God and God is in us; a great mystical conception, staggering to the human mind and yet a reality which can only be expressed in some such term as this—sharing.

The second thing is that as well as being partakers of God, we are partners with Him, sharers in His interests and in His great purposes. That means that we have become interested in the sense of being partners in God's great plan of salvation, in His attitude towards life in this world and in all His wonderful provision for it. Now we who are in Christ have entered into that; that again is something which is emphasised everywhere in the pages of the New Testament, and it is a good test of our whole Christian position. It seems to me that by this definition we cannot truly be Christians unless we are really interested in God's enterprise in this world.

In other words, we know what it is to be grieved by the sin of this world; we do not merely look at the world with a political eye or with a social eye or with an eye of beneficence. No, we see things as God Himself sees them. Evil becomes a reality, sin becomes a reality in the new sense, and we see these powers, these evil forces that are in the world and which are manipulating the life of the world in their enmity against God and we are concerned about that. We feel that God is in it and that we are likewise in it, in that we are concerned to bring the purposes of God to pass. We meditate, we pray; we do everything that we are capable of in furthering the kingdom of light, so that the kingdom of evil may be finally routed. We are sharers in God's thought and in God's enterprise and in God's whole interest in this life and world.

Then let me add something about the second great aspect of this which is the most blessed and comforting and consoling thought for every true Christian. Fellowship always means communion, it always means intercourse, it always means, if you like, conversation—sharing. We talk about having fellowship with people, and that is quite right; it is part of the essential meaning of the word and of its Christian meaning in particular. 'We had a wonderful time of fellowship together,' somebody says, having had conversation with somebody else, and it means that—not only sharing in common but talking about it—this element of communion.

Let us analyse this a bit further. 'Our fellowship is with the Father', and I mean by that that I have communion with God. Now this can be looked at in two ways. First of all it can be looked at from our side, then it can be looked at from God's side. What does this wondrous thing which has been made possible for us in Christ mean from our side? It means, obviously and of necessity, that we have come to know God. God is no longer a stranger somewhere away in the heavens; He is no longer some stray force or power somewhere, some supreme energy. God is no longer some potentate or lawgiver far removed and away from us; God now is someone whom we know.

Consider the Apostle Paul especially as he deals with this; you will find that in writing to the Galatians he talks about their knowing God; 'but now, after that ye have known God, or rather are known of God' (Gal 4:9)—that is the idea. God is now a reality; we know Him, and that is the very essence of this matter. You cannot have communion, you cannot have conversation with a person without knowing that person—there is nothing distant, there is an intimacy and a knowledge.

The Christian, says John, is one who has come to know God, but it is not only that. God not only is a great person—I speak with reverence—the Christian is one who has come to know God as Father. That is why John uses his terms so carefully—'our fellowship is with the Father.' The Christian is one who turns to God and addresses Him as 'Abba, Father'; that is how Paul puts it in Romans 8:15—this spirit of adoption, the result of which is that we know God in that intimate way so that we address Him as 'Abba, Father' because we are His children. So it means that of necessity, but not only that. It also means that we delight in God and that we have joy in His presence. We know God in that way.

But then I think that we can go on to say this: to have communion with God means that we desire to speak with Him and that we have the ability to do that. Let me put it like this: All of us have known what it is to have difficulty in connection with prayer. It is not very difficult to talk to a person whom we love in this world, is it? When we love someone there is no need to try to make conversation, it flows freely; we love that person, and everything in us is stimulated. That is the characteristic of true fellowship and communion. But we all know what it is to get on our knees and to find ourselves speechless, to have nothing to say.

Now if this is our state and condition we do not know God as we ought; true fellowship with God means we desire, we delight in speaking to Him and we have a desire to praise Him. If we love someone, we want to tell him so; we not only say it in actions, we want to say it in words and we do say it. And it is exactly the same with God. The one who is in true relationship with Him praises Him. We do not come to God because we want something. No, rather, we enjoy coming to Him; it is the greatest thing for us—this is the whole idea in this word 'communion'.

Another way is to put it like this: men and women who are in communion with God are those who are sure of the presence of God. I have had people say to me, 'I get on my knees, but I do not feel that God is there'; and you cannot have communion if that is your feeling. No, those who are in communion know that God is there, they realise His presence, it is an essential part of this whole position of fellowship.

Then, of course, all this leads to confidence in speaking to God, in taking our petitions and requests and desires to Him. In other words one of the best ways in which we can test whether we are truly in fellowship and communion with God is to examine our prayer life. How much prayer life is there in my life? How often do I pray; do I find freedom in prayer, do I delight in prayer, or is prayer a wearisome task; do I never know enlargement and liberty in it? For what we are told here is that the Christian in Christ has been brought into fellowship and communion with God, and as you read the psalmists you will find that they enjoyed it, to them it was the supreme thing. Read the statements in the New Testament, read the lives of the saints and of those who have gone before us—that is the characteristic, that is the possibility—conversation with God, an enjoyment of it and a delight in it.

But now let me say just a word on the other side, for as we have seen, there are always two sides in fellowship. 'Truly our fellowship is with the Father, and with his Son Jesus Christ.' How do I know that? I know it because He gives me tokens of His presence and a sense of His nearness. We have said that communion means realising the presence of God, and there is the basic minimum in this matter, that those who can claim that they are in communion with God and say they have fellowship with Him must be able to say, 'I have known that I was in the presence of God who graciously gives me tokens of this; He gives me manifestations.' You can see the dangerous thing I am saying, how it opens the door to fanaticism and excesses; but we have no fellowship with God unless in some way we have known that He was there, that He gave His gracious intimation of His nearness and His presence. He also speaks in His own way to the soul, not always with an audible voice, but He speaks. He gives us consolation, He creates within us holy desires and longings; it is He who does that.

Paul said in writing to the Philippians, 'For it is God which worketh in you both to will and to do of His good pleasure' (Phil 2:13). That is the way to have fellowship with God. You are aware of the surging of those holy desires, and you say to yourself, 'It is God; it is God speaking to me; it is God saying something and calling forth a response in me.' 'We love him, because he first loved us,' says John later in this epistle, and God has fellowship with us in that way.

Not only that, He reveals His will to us. He show us what He would have us to do; He leads us, He opens doors and shuts them; sometimes He puts up barriers and obstacles. You know what I am speaking about. It means that you are aware of the fact that you are in the hands of God and that He is dealing with you, and that as you go forward in this journey called life, God is there. Sometimes the door is shut and you cannot understand it. You say, 'I wanted to go there, but I cannot' and then you say, 'But God is with me and He has shut the door.' Then suddenly you find the door opened and you know it is the One who is walking with you who has suddenly opened it. That is having fellowship with God, knowing that He is there in these various ways in which He manipulates our lives and speaks to us and gives us wisdom and understanding. Every one of these things contains a danger; they all need to be carefully qualified, and yet they are essential to fellowship and communion.

Then He supplies us with strength according to our need and according to our situation. You will find all these things if you read Christian literature; how the saints have been enabled to re-enact what our Lord Himself experienced. Towards the end, He said in effect to the disciples, 'You are all going to leave Me, you will all run away and turn your backs upon Me; in a few hours you will leave Me alone. And yet,' He said, 'I am not alone, for the Father is with Me' (Jn 16:32). And His last words on the cross were: 'Father, into thy hands I commend my spirit' (Lk 23:46). God was there with Him, and the saints all repeat that in their lives and in their experiences. Consider their deathbed testimonies. They will tell you, many of them, how glorious and wonderful it was, that even there they had this fellowship. They were not alone, the presence was there; they could not see God, they could not hear an audible voice, but they knew God was there filling the very atmosphere; they were more certain of God than of anyone else.

Truly, certainly, astoundingly, astonishingly our fellowship is with the Father. Enoch walked with God, and if we are truly Christian, we should be walking with God, speaking to Him, knowing He is there speaking to us, delighting to praise Him, anxious to know Him more and more. Let us test ourselves by this. It is not enough to be orthodox. That is essential, but it is not enough; the vital question for us all to put to ourselves is as simple as this— do I know God?

8

Mysticism

And truly our fellowship is with the
Father, and with his Son Jesus Christ.

1 JOHN 1:3

We have been seeing together that this is really the great offer which is held out to us by the gospel of our Lord Jesus Christ. It is the one thing, the supreme thing that is held before us as that which can enable us to live in a world which, as we have seen so abundantly in the Scriptures, is essentially opposed to God and opposed, therefore, to all who belong to Him. 'If the world hate you, ye know that it hated me before it hated you,' said our Lord in John 15:18, and that is something which as Christian people we should never lose sight of–that the world in its outlook and mentality is opposed to God, and until it becomes converted, until it receives a new life, that will remain its condition.

So the problem confronting us is, how are we to live this Christian, this godly life in a world that is so antagonistic to us in every respect? And the answer of this epistle, as it is the answer of the whole of the New Testament, is that there is only one way in which this can be done, and that is to have this fellowship with God; and that, according to John, is the astounding thing which our Lord came to do; not only to reveal it to us, but to make it possible for us. That is the great emphasis. It is not only a teaching, it is more than a teaching; it is something which He actually does for us.

Now we have been considering this great statement from certain angles; we have been considering certain things that had to take place before it could be possible—the work of Christ—and then we have tried to look at it directly in order to remind ourselves of what exactly it means. But in doing that I have constantly had to utter a word of warning. There is no subject, I think we will all agree, which has led to more misunderstanding perhaps than just this particular question. The whole idea is so exalted and wonderful that once we realise that it is a possibility at all, we must immediately be concerned about having and experiencing it; and in some senses the history of the Church can be described as the history of the various ways in which men and women have tried to arrive at and maintain this communion, this fellowship with God. Some of the greatest adorations in Christian experience have been the result of this particular interest and particular endeavour, so that it is a subject which we must examine rather carefully. There are false ways in which we could seek this fellowship with God as well as true ones.

Now it is impossible to deal with them all, so it seems to me that the most convenient thing to do is to show the two main ways in which men have sought fellowship with God—the evangelical way and the mystical way. That is a pretty general classification. There are many instances in Christian biographies of men and women who seem more or less to combine the two ways, shading one off against the other. There are many sub-divisions of the mystical way, and clearly we cannot hope to deal with them in one discourse. It would take a whole series of discourses. There are large volumes written on many of them; indeed one could say that there are libraries on this whole question of mysticism. It is a most fascinating and absorbing and indeed a most thrilling matter. Clearly I can therefore only deal with what I may describe as the essence of the evangelical position and the essence of the mystical view. (If I may in passing recommend a book that is, I think, one of the most valuable and instructive in this respect, it is a series of lectures that were delivered in 1928 and published under the title of *The Vision of God*, written by Kenneth E. Kirk.)

Here, then, is a subject which must engage our attention, because the mystical and the evangelical in certain respects are so similar, and that is where, perhaps, the danger comes in. The mystic and the evangelical both agree that God does deal directly with our spirits and gives us a knowledge of Himself. They are both agreed that fellowship is not something formal and that the true Christian position is not merely something external and mechanical. The mystic and the evangelical agree that our object and endeavour should be fellowship with God; neither of them is content merely with discharging a certain amount of responsibility, or of conformity to certain moral standards. That, they say, is not the thing; the world can do that, and so can other religions. No, they say, the special thing about the Christian religion is that it offers a man fellowship, an intimacy, a knowledge of God, and they are both concerned with obtaining it.

But as I want to try to show you, it is in the way in which they seek to do this that they tend to part company. Again I would remind you that there have been certain cases where really one must grant that the people concerned have been evangelical and mystical at the same time. There are cases of people who were sufficiently evangelical to see the dangers of their own mysticism, but that does make it rather difficult from the standpoint of classification. Let me give you one example. Take Bernard of Clairvaux. He was clearly mystical and yet we must grant he was evangelical, and there have been other examples of the same thing. There is a great deal of the mystic in Charles Wesley, although he was primarily evangelical, and the same can be said of his brother John. There are such cases which seem to be difficult to classify, so let us deal, therefore, with the big principles.

What is this whole idea of seeking fellowship and communion with God along the pathway of what is described as mysticism? There are, as we have said, many sub-divisions of mysticism. It can be entirely non-Christian; many of the Greek pagan philosophers were mystics in the true sense of the word; there are pagan mystics, as well as religious ones, and as well as, in a sense, Christian mystics. There are certain things which are common to them all; they believe in general that a man can have a kind of immediate intuition of the infinite and the eternal. One definition of the word is: 'Mysticism is the belief that God may be known face to face without anything intervening; the direct knowledge and awareness of God.' Or perhaps better still: 'Mysticism is the theory that the purity and blessedness to be derived from communion with God are not to be obtained from the Scriptures and the use of the ordinary means of grace, but by a supernatural and immediate divine influence, which influence is to be secured by the simple yielding of the soul without thought or effort to the divine influence.'

Generally, we can put it like this, that mysticism makes *feeling* the source of knowledge of God, and not intellect, not reason, not understanding. That is really the differentiating thing about mysticism. The mystic is one who says that this knowledge of God is not something one obtains as the result of understanding or any external objective knowledge; it is something immediate, a direct traffic between one's heart and the Spirit of God Himself, and it happens primarily in the realm of the feelings. God makes known truth to the mystic in some shape or form.

Now that is the big difficulty to the evangelical approach to this subject. The evangelical always asserts the primacy of the Word of God, objective revelation; the mystic tends to depreciate that and says, 'No, what I have to do is somehow or other just submit myself, and upon my spirit in this passive state God will do something by means of my sensations and susceptibilities, and I will come to know God.' Its primacy and emphasis is upon the sensibility rather than upon the understanding.

Now not all mystics are concerned about the same thing. I do not want to spend time with technical terms, but there are three main types. There are what you can call the *theopathic*, the mystic who is concerned about pure feeling and sensation. Then there is the *theosophic*–people who call themselves 'theosophists' today and who are concerned about a knowledge of God resulting from experience and want to examine their knowledge. And there is the *theurgic*, the man who is interested in phenomena, who is anxious to have visions and strange phenomenal experiences; the kind of mystic who delights in seeing balls of light, or illuminations, and likes to talk about trances and 'feeling' the power of God.

Now it is interesting to glance at the history of mysticism. It almost invariably comes in as a protest against a sort of formalism and deadness in the Church. You get this quite as much in the Roman Catholic Church as you do in Protestantism, indeed more so. I think that is very significant in and of itself; the Roman Catholics have always produced more mystics than the Protestants. Mysticism is also a protest against rationalism and a tendency to over-intellectualise the Christian faith. Thus you will find that mysticism has generally tended to show itself at certain periods in the history of the Church. In the early centuries of the Church when there was a good deal of discussion about Christian doctrine and when the doctors of the Church spent their time in working out the arguments against Greek philosophy in order to safeguard the Christian faith, the danger was that the whole gospel might be turned into an intellectual system. And it was at that point that the first Christian mystics came into being. 'We must be careful,' they said; 'With all our definitions, we are in danger of losing the life.' So mysticism, in a sense, began in the early centuries in Egypt, as a protest against the mere intellectualising of the Christian faith and a kind of formality in the Church.

Then you had another great outbreak of mysticism in the Middle Ages with Bernard and people like that, and again it followed very definitely from the same cause. There was a danger that the Roman Catholic Church of that time was attempting to produce a formal school of philosophy. It had become materialistic and dead and lifeless, and there were certain men, even in the Roman Catholic Church in those dark Middle Ages, who began to say to themselves and to one another, 'We are losing the life; the business of the Christian faith is to bring men into a knowledge of God; here are learned philosophers arguing about the exact nature of angels and how many angels can be suspended at the same time on the point of a nail and all these wonderful philosophical abstracts. That in itself,' they said, 'is a denial of the Christian faith.' So you had an outbreak of mysticism in the Middle Ages just as you had it in the first century.

There is the evidence of this in Protestantism as well. The Reformation came in the sixteenth century and, of course, it led to a great realisation of a kind of spiritual power. But, as almost invariably happens after a revival, it was followed by a period of deadness. Then you came to the age of the theologians, and again there were some people who began to feel that the life had been lost, that this excellent theology had somehow or other become mechanical, and there was a reaction in the direction of mysticism. People of the Puritan period began to put a new emphasis upon the Holy Spirit, and one of the manifestations of the emphasis was what has come to be known as Quakerism.

Here again are mystics, and theirs was a protest against this over-intellectuality of the Christian faith or a merely mechanical statement of certain teaching. So you get the main manifestations of mysticism in Protestantism amongst the Quakers and the others at the end of the seventeenth and the beginning of the eighteenth centuries. One of the most outstanding of these in this country [UK] was William Law with his book *The Serious Call*. Now he had a great influence upon the brothers Wesley, and he was the man who was used of God to bring them into the light and the truth.

Mysticism, then, is concerned to put emphasis upon the reality of the knowledge of God and communion with Him. How does it do so? I have already indicated its method in general, although here again there are two main schools amongst the mystics. The first school believes in quietism, pure passivity. They say you have nothing to do but to be quiet and to relax; this teaching is still popular in various quarters. 'You must not try to think,' they say; 'you must not try to make any endeavour; what you must do is to abandon yourself to God and God will then speak to you and do things to you and you will come to this knowledge of Him'—passivity and quietism. The great exponent of this particular aspect was the famous French woman, Madame Guyon.

That is one way, but there is another type of mystic who is most active. It is most unjust and unfair to think of the mystic as some sort of vague, nebulous kind of person. Someone once said that we must not, if we want to be fair to mysticism, confuse it with the mystical. There is a type of mysticism that is most active, and it says that this vision splendid and this knowledge of God is only to be obtained by a very rigid discipline. You must indulge in introspection, you must examine yourself; then you must go on to meditation; you must think about these things and then you must go on to the stage of where, having meditated and examined yourself, you have a kind of intuition of God. That is what is called 'the mystic way', which calls upon you to purge yourself from sin, and then you may have to go through a period of what is known as 'the dark night of the soul' when you feel you do not know God. But you just remain quiet and you go on with your introspection and meditation and your ascetic practices, and if you do so you will come out into a state of illumination, you will begin to see the truth. You will begin to come to a state when you know, and then you will just have to contemplate, and ultimately you will arrive in a state of union with God when you have more or less lost yourself altogether.

You will find that these mystics have been very active people; their one endeavour has been to come to know God. Most of the men who left life in the world and became monks and anchorites and who went into monasteries were concerned with nothing but that. They put on camel-hair shirts, they deliberately mutilated their bodies, as it were, believing that was the way that would lead ultimately to this state of union with God; and as a result of all this they claimed various experiences. You hear about raptures and visions of joy.

Now what is the evangelical criticism of all this? Let me tabulate it in this way. The main criticism of the evangelical to all this can be put in this form: It is a claim to a continuation of inspiration. The mystic in a sense is claiming that God is dealing as directly with him as He was with the Old Testament prophets; he claims God is dealing with him as He did with the Apostles. Now we as evangelicals believe that God gave a message to the prophets, He gave a message to the Apostles; but we say that because God has done that, it is unnecessary that He should do that directly with us. I do not claim that what I am speaking here has been given to me by a direct inspiration of God. I am here to expound the Scriptures. I claim that the Holy Spirit enables me to do so, but I am not claiming that I have received a direct message from God. No, this is the message, the message that was given to John and his fellow Apostles; I have entered into fellowship with the Apostles and I am repeating their message. But the mystic says he has received a new and fresh message and that he is in a state of direct inspiration.

My second criticism would be that mysticism of necessity puts the Scriptures on one side and makes them more or less unnecessary. You will always find that persons who have a mystical tendency never talk very much about the Bible. They do not read it very much; indeed I think you will find that this is true of most mystical people. They say, 'No, I do not follow the Bible reading schemes; I find one verse is generally enough for me. I take one verse and then I begin to meditate.' That is typical of the mystic. He does not need this objective revelation; he wants something to start him in his meditation and he will then receive it as coming directly from God; he depreciates the value of the Scriptures.

Indeed, I do not hesitate to go further and say that mysticism, as a whole, even tends to make our Lord Himself unnecessary. That is a very serious statement, but I am prepared to substantiate it. There have been people who have been mystical and who claim that their souls have immediate access to God. They say that just as they are, they have but to relax and let go and let God speak to them and He will do so; they do not mention the Lord Jesus Christ.

Not only that, I think we can put it like this. The danger of mysticism is to concentrate so much on the Lord's work *in* us that it forgets the Lord's work *for* us. In other words, it is so concerned about this immediate work upon the soul that it quite forgets the preliminary work that had to be done before anything could be done upon the soul. It tends to forget the cross and the absolute necessity of the atoning death of Christ before fellowship with God is in any way possible.

Or indeed we can go further and put that in a different way. Mysticism is never very strong on the doctrine of sin. The mystic tends to come and say, 'Look here, you have nothing to worry about. If you want to know God just as you are, you have to start getting into communion with Him, and He will speak to you and will give you all the blessings.' They never mention the doctrine of sin in the sense that the guilt of sin is such a terrible thing that nothing but the coming of the Son of God into the world and the bearing of our sins in His own body on the cross could ever enable God to speak to the soul.

Another very serious criticism of mysticism is that it always leaves us without a standard. Let us imagine I follow the mystic way. I begin to have experiences; I think God is speaking to me; how do I know it is God who is speaking to me? How can I know I am not speaking to man; how can I be sure that I am not the victim of hallucinations, since this has happened to many of the mystics? If I believe in mysticism as such without the Bible, how do I test my experiences? How do I prove the Scriptures; how do I know I am not perhaps being deluded by Satan as an angel of light in order to keep me from the true and living God? I have no standard.

Or in other words, my last criticism is that mysticism always tends to fanaticism and excesses. If you put feelings before understanding, you are bound to end in that, because you have nothing to check your experiences with, and you will have no reason to control your sensations and susceptibilities.

'Very well,' says someone, 'if that is your criticism of mysticism, what is the evangelical way in order that I may come to this knowledge and fellowship with God?' It is quite simple, and it is this: It always starts with the Scriptures; it says that the Scriptures are my only authority and final standard with regard to these matters, with regard to a knowledge of God. The evangelical doctrine tells me not to look into myself but to look into the Word of God; not to examine myself, but to look at the revelation that has been given to me. It tells me that God can only be known in His own way, the way which has been revealed in the Scriptures themselves.

I must start with Christ's work for me. There is no true knowledge of God without Christ. 'No man cometh unto the Father, but by me,' said our Lord (Jn 14:6). I must come by Christ, and I must come via the cross. Christ's teaching cannot bring me to God because there is the guilt of my sin. It is Christ's work for me before Christ's work in me; it is what He has done objectively there in that transaction, before He can do anything upon my soul.

So I start with that, and then I believe that having dealt with the guilt of my sin He gives me life. It is a gift from God; it is not something of which I can say I can attain to by following the mystic way; eternal life is the gift of God, and I must realise that it only comes to me on the condition that having seen my sinfulness I believe on the Lord Jesus Christ and thereby trust Him for reconciliation. And therefore as eternal life is the gift of God, I must not seek it directly; it is something that will come to me as the result of following after God. Our Lord put it perfectly once and for ever in the Sermon on the Mount. He did not say, 'Blessed are they who hunger and thirst after spiritual experiences, blessed are they who hunger and thirst after joy and happiness'—not at all! The blessed, the ones who experience a blessing, 'hunger and thirst after *righteousness*: for they shall be filled' (Mt 5:6).

We must not seek this great thing directly; you and I are to seek righteousness and if we do, God will give us the blessing. This wonderful experience of fellowship with the Father and with His Son Jesus Christ is something that He gives to all who truly seek Him in the way He has taught us. It is the whole theme of this first epistle of John; the way to obtain this fellowship, this wondrous experience, is to read this Word, not to take a verse and then fit it into my mystical meditation. No, it is objective revelation, the facts of the incarnation, the life, the miracles, the death, the resurrection, the facts of salvation—'These things,' says John, 'which we have seen and witnessed; these proofs which we have touched and felt and handled.'

The evangelical way of fellowship with God, therefore, is to come straight to the Word, to know its truth, to believe it and to accept it—to pray on this basis and to exert our whole being in an effort and an endeavour to live it and to practise it. 'Blessed are they which do hunger and thirst after righteousness: for they shall be filled'; filled with the fullness of God, with the knowledge of God and such blessings as God alone can give.

Mysticism is an attempt at a short cut to the great experiences; the way of the Scriptures is the other way—simple, indirect but certain, and free from the effects of fanaticism and excesses and leading to a balanced Christian life and living, true to God and His Word, in line with the Apostles and in line with the mighty evangelical tradition throughout the ages and the centuries. May the Lord in His mercy open our eyes to the dangers of these side paths and to all the excesses and fanaticism which ultimately bring disrepute upon the Lord and His great salvation, and keep us ever always to that simplicity which is in Christ Jesus.

9

The Holiness of God

This then is the message which we have heard of him, and declare unto you, that God is light, and in him is no darkness at all.

1 JOHN 1:5

Here in this verse we begin the consideration of the various reasons and causes which John gives his readers for the fact that the fellowship of Christian people with God is not as full as it should be, and is so frequently interrupted. He has announced his great theme, he has reminded them of the great good news, that what is offered to the Christian in this life and world is fellowship with the Father and with His Son, Jesus Christ, or if you like, through His Son Jesus Christ. The Apostle is not concerned in this particular matter to deal with the person of the Lord as such; he has already done that in his Gospel. Not only that, these people, being members of the Christian Church, have already been taught that; John is rather taking it for granted. What he is concerned about here is to enable them to continue in the grace of the Lord Jesus Christ. He is anxious to show them the fullness of this fellowship which is offered and how this fellowship may be maintained in spite of various hindrances and obstacles.

When we gave a general analysis of this letter, we pointed out how that is the scheme on which he works. There are certain things which tend to interfere with the fellowship or to rob us of this true fullness, and immediately he comes to one of them, one of the things which we all so constantly tend to forget. Indeed, here in this verse he holds us face to face with one of the most vital and common things of all. There can be no doubt about that from any standpoint and especially, as I hope to show you, from what can be described as the theological standpoint, there is no more important verse than this one. It immediately concentrates our attention on something that is quite fundamental and primary, and if we neglect it or fail to understand it as we ought, we must of necessity find ourselves overwhelmed with troubles. And therefore we can, perhaps, best consider it together by putting it in the form of a number of propositions.

The first principle is this: we must always start with God. You see how John plunges into this without any introduction; indeed there is something almost surprising about the way in which he does it. He has already said in verse 4, 'And these things write we unto you, that your joy may be full.' Very well, says John, 'this, then is the message which we have heard of him and declare unto you, that God is light and in him is no darkness at all.' The starting point, let me repeat, always must be God Himself.

Now it may sound strange to some that we take the trouble to put that in the form of a principle. 'Surely,' someone may feel like arguing, 'that is something that is self-evident and obvious. Surely the very first and basic thing for Christian people is that they should start with God.' And yet I want to suggest that half our troubles arise in the Christian life because we do not start at this point. It is because we tend to assume that we know the truth about God, it is because we tend to assume that everything is all right in our ideas about God that many, if not most, of our problems occur, because we constantly start not with God but with ourselves. So many people assume that they believe in God and that therefore they need not be concerned about examining their belief. 'I have always believed in God,' says someone, 'it has never occurred to me not to believe in Him.' So in all their thought about these things they tend not to start with God, because they assume that; rather, they tend to start with themselves.

This, of course, has been the outstanding source of trouble

since roughly 1860. It had started before that, but it has been particularly true since that time. Man has been put in the centre, and
all thinking and all philosophising has tended to start with man; he
has been placed at the centre of the universe. Man, if you like, has
been placed on the throne and everything, God included, has had
to be put in terms of man. Man has set himself up as an authority;
it is man and his ideas that count; it is always man in his need and
condition that seems to be the starting point.

Now that is the very initial error and the source of most mis-
understandings. The Bible is constantly reminding us that we must
start with God. If ever I start with man, I must ultimately go wrong
in all my thinking about truth; because if I start there, everything
accommodates itself to my doctrine of man. Yet the doctrine of the
Bible is that I can never know man truly unless I look at him in the
sight of God and in the teaching concerning God.

So I must always be careful not to start with myself. It is very
difficult not to do so; our whole approach to the gospel and to
Christianity naturally tends to be from that self-centred and selfish
standpoint. We argue like this: Here I am in this world with its troubles and I am ill at ease. I am looking for something I have not got.
I am aware of my needs and desires; I am aware of a lack of happiness, and the tendency for most of us is to approach the whole
subject of religion, to approach God and Christian truth and everything else, in terms of my desires and my demands. What has He
to say to me and to give to me? What can I get out of this Christian
faith and religion? Is there something in this that is going to ease
my problems and help me in this dark and difficult world?

But that, according to this verse and indeed according to the
whole of the Bible, is the root source of error, it is the initial fallacy,
it is indeed almost blasphemy against God. The first answer of the
gospel can always, in effect, be put in this way: 'Forget yourself and
contemplate God.' This, then, is 'the message which we have heard
of him'; not that your needs and mine can suddenly be met by the
gospel, but rather that 'God is light, and in him is no darkness at
all.' Immediately we start with God and not with ourselves.

Furthermore, this is a very valuable test of any teaching or of
any doctrine which may confront us. You will find that the great

characteristic of the cults and of every religion which is not the true Christian faith is that they tend to come to us in terms of our need. That is why they are always so popular and so successful; they seem to be giving us the thing we want. We have our needs, and they seem to offer us everything just as we want it without any pain or difficulty. There is no more thorough-going test, therefore, of the truth of the faith and of the religion that we may be concerned with than this.

Primarily, the initial test, the characteristic of the revelation of the Bible, the first crucible, in a sense, of the Christian faith, is that it starts with God. We are silenced, we are put into the background, we are not considering man first and foremost. It is God, it all starts with Him–'In the beginning, God'–and He is at the centre. The very term *theology* should remind us of that. Theology does not mean knowledge concerning man; primarily it is knowledge of God.

So this is of supreme importance to us as we come to consider the whole question of fellowship and walking with God and of enjoying the life of God. Most of our troubles are due to our self-centredness and concern for ourselves. The psychologists are aware of that and they have their own way of dealing with it, but they do not really meet the situation and the problem. They are only temporarily successful, because the whole time they are pandering to this self within us. No, the way to be delivered from self-centredness is to stand in the presence of God.

According to the Bible the initial cause of man's ills is that, having been created in the likeness and image of God, instead of living a life in subservience to God, man, alas, suddenly exalted himself and claimed a kind of equality with God; and it is his own self-assertion that has led to all his perplexities. Is not the position in which we find ourselves the same situation as that of the people who have gone before us in all ages and at all times? We begin to see that our fallacy is to exaggerate our own twentieth century with its problems. We see we are paying too much attention to our environment and conditions, and we suddenly come back and face this ultimate, absolute truth–that we are all ultimately in the presence of God.

The starting point, then, always must be God and not ourselves and our needs, our desires and our happiness. Before the Bible begins to talk to us about our particular needs, it would have us see ourselves in the sight of God. Its approach to the whole situation is quite unique and entirely different. It does not say it can aid and help us; it confronts us with its own truth, its message from God which comes down to us.

Let me elaborate that a little more. Having reminded us that we must start with God, our text reminds us in the second place that we must accept the revelation concerning God which we have in the Bible and primarily in the person of the Lord Jesus Christ. 'This then is the message which we have heard of him, and declare unto you, that God is light, and in him is no darkness at all.' It is not enough, in other words, for us to say that we must always start with God. The vital question is: what is the truth concerning God; who is God; what is God; what do we know about Him?

Here again I think we see at once that we are face to face with another of those primary, fundamental questions, and it is tragic to have to remind ourselves of how it is always with regard to these very things that we go astray. 'Oh yes,' people say, 'I have always believed in God.' There are only a very few who actually say they do not believe in God. The average man says, 'Yes, of course I do', and then if you ask him what his ideas of God are—or indeed you need not ask him because he is so fond of expressing his opinions!— he says, 'If God is a God of love, I cannot understand why He should allow conditions like these present ones to exist. Why does God allow wars, why does God . . . ?' Immediately, you see, he is telling you what he thinks of God.

That again, according to the Bible, is one of the first fallacies. To believe in God we must accept the revelation concerning Him, and that revelation is only to be found in the Bible. Now that is a dogmatic assertion, and so is the verse which we are considering. 'This then is the message,' says John, 'which we have heard of him, and declare—announce, proclaim—unto you.' John does not say, 'This is the sort of picture I have of God'; he does not say, 'As the result of much thought and meditation and reading, and as the result of my study of the Greek philosophies and contemporary thought, this is the idea I have now arrived at concerning God.' Not at all! He goes out of his way to say the exact opposite.

John says, 'What I am telling you is what my fellow Apostles and I heard from Him and heard about Him.' He has already referred to the Lord Jesus Christ as 'that which was from the beginning, which we have heard and seen and looked upon.' He had to start with Him, 'because,' he says in effect, 'in fact I did not know God and my ideas concerning Him were false until I met Him, until I heard Him and companied with Him for three years. I heard His words; He said on one occasion, "He that hath seen me hath seen the Father. You have been with me and have you not known me, have you not seen and heard me?" He is my authority,' says John; 'He told us certain things and I am just repeating what He said.'

That is the biblical position; so in other words we come to what we may call the watershed in this matter. There are only two ultimate positions; we either regard the Bible as authoritative, or else we trust to human ideas, to what is called philosophy. The whole case of the Bible is that this is the unique revelation of God and that finally I am shut up and shut into this particular revelation.

This again has been a matter which has often engaged the minds and the attention of God's people. What are the so-called proofs or the philosophical arguments for the being and existence of God? Now, according to the Bible I think we must look at it like this: these things have their place and yet they are not ultimately the final source of truth. Reason can take me to a certain point, and it is quite right to use it up to that point, but that will never bring me to a true knowledge of God. I can argue about the being of God in a purely philosophical manner; I can say that every effect has a cause, and that cause in its turn is but the effect of another cause, and I can go back and back until I come to the ultimate cause and that must be God. Well, that is all right as far as it goes, but to believe that is not to know God.

Again, I can use a moral argument; I can say that I observe in life that there is bad, good and better; does that not imply that there must be a best somewhere? Moral arguments lead to arguments about the absolute, and that is God. This too is all right as far as it goes, it is quite sound, it is perfectly cogent, and yet when I have worked out that argument and accepted it, I do not know God in the sense that John means here. What John tells us is that we can have fellowship with the Father and with His Son, Jesus Christ.

I can use the cosmological argument; I can assert an intellectual argument as to my existence and my being and show that yet there must be some ultimate source of this being. Again, all this is quite sound philosophically, but that is not to know God. No, these arguments, these so-called proofs of the being and existence of God are all right as far as they go, but they do not bring me to an ultimate knowledge, to a communion, to the fellowship which is offered me in the gospel of the Lord Jesus Christ.

Here I am left ultimately in this position of relying upon the revelation, and this is the challenging effect of faith; faith calls upon us to come to this truth as little children, acknowledging our failure, acknowledging our incompetence and impotence, and it confronts us by these declarations, these announcements, and it asks us to accept this truth. I cannot know God ultimately apart from the revelation that He has been pleased to give me of Himself; I cannot know God ultimately in the sense of truly having fellowship with Him except in the Lord Jesus Christ.

Our Lord said, 'I am the way, the truth, and the life: no man cometh unto the Father, but by me' (Jn 14:6). Now I wonder what happens exactly when we test ourselves by that particular statement. Have we found the Lord Jesus Christ absolutely essential in that way, or have we held some view of God which has made us believe we can find God whenever we seek for Him or that we can arrive at God by our own efforts? Our Lord put it like that, and that is the Christian position: 'No man cometh unto the Father, but by me.' He is essential, and we cannot know God truly except we believe this revelation concerning Him. And that is exactly what John says: 'This is the message which we have heard of him and which we declare unto you.' 'I believed things about God,' says John, 'before I met Him. I had ideas concerning God, but when I met Him and listened to Him and knew Him, it was only then I really came to know God.' As Martin Luther put it in his own blunt and striking manner, 'I know no God but Jesus Christ.'

Now there is something, surely, we all must confess, that tends to come to us in rather a startling way. Our tendency is to say that we are all right in our belief of God, but the trouble is our belief in Jesus Christ. But the question is, what has the Christian faith to offer us by way of salvation; and the answer is that it is our thoughts of God that are ultimately wrong; it is in our approach to Him that we go astray; we must start with Him, and we are confined entirely to the revelation which has been given to us. He gave it to the patriarchs of old; He gave it in the Ten Commandments and the moral law and He gave it in the prophets whom He raised up one after another. All these were intended to give us knowledge and understanding of God, but it is only in the incarnate Son that we really come to *know* Him; it is only there that we can possibly know Him as Father and truly have fellowship with Him.

Then the next proposition is that we must start with the holiness of God. There again, surely this fifth verse must come to us as rather a surprise. Surely our first reaction when we read it is to feel it is almost a contradiction. John has just been saying, 'These things write we unto you, that your joy may be full'; so, how is it to be full? Well, 'This then is the message which we have heard of him, and declare unto you, that God is . . .' What would you have expected there? I suggest that most of us would have expected, 'God is love, God is mercy, God is compassion'; but the startling and astonishing thing is that he says, 'God is light, and in him is no darkness at all.' And we want to say to John, 'Have you forgotten what you have been saying? You have been saying that we are to be given an amazing joy, and then you confront us with that.'

But that is precisely what he does say. In other words, we must not start with the power of God or with the greatness of God, though they are perfectly true. We must not start with the knowledge of God, though that is absolutely essential. Nor must we start with God as a source of philosophy. We must not even start with God as love.

Now we can see at once how by putting it like this we just give an utter contradiction to what has been so popular especially, again, since 1860; the great message that has been preached for a hundred years is 'God is love'. That is the thing that has been emphasised, and we have been told that our fathers, and especially the Puritans with their preaching about justice and righteousness and repentance and sin and punishment and death, had been entirely contradicting and denying the gospel of Jesus Christ. We have been told that God is love—that is what we wanted and there He was to meet us; yet what an utter travesty of the gospel that is! This is the message: 'God is light, and in him is no darkness at all.'

I say it with reverence that before I begin to think and consider the love of God and the mercy and compassion of God, I must start with the holiness of God. I go further; unless I start with the holiness of God, my whole conception of the love of God is going to be false, and this of course is what we have been witnessing. We have had the flabby, sentimental notions of God as a God of love, always smiling upon us, and then when wars and calamities come we are baffled and we turn our backs upon religion—this is what millions have been doing since the great wars of this century. And the trouble has actually been due to the fact that they did not start the way the Scriptures start, with the holiness of God. God is utter, absolute righteousness and justice; 'holiness, without which no man shall see the Lord' (Heb 12:14); 'God is a consuming fire' (Heb 12:29); sharing in the light that is unapproachable, everlasting and eternal in the brightness and the perfection of His absolute qualities. Light! And light must not be interpreted as knowledge; light is knowledge, but light essentially stands here for holiness—utter, absolute holiness and purity. And John makes certain that we shall not go astray in our interpretation, by adding this negative: 'And in him is no darkness at all.'

Now it is interesting to observe how the commentators, and even some of the best of them, during the last hundred years, as the result of a modern philosophical approach, are so anxious to interpret this term 'light' in terms of knowledge and truth and enlightenment and understanding. But that is not it; it includes that, but essentially it is the character of God, and the character of God is His holiness.

But why is all this so essential? 'Why,' asks someone, 'is it so vital that we must start with God and not ourselves; why do we start with God and not with our opinions? Why must I be so attuned to this revelation? Why must I start with the holiness of God rather than with His love?'

Let me give you some answers. I suggest that if you do not start with the holiness of God you will never understand God's plan of salvation, which is that salvation is only possible to us through the death of our Lord Jesus Christ on the cross on Calvary's hill. But the question arises; why is that cross essential, why is that the only way whereby man can be saved? If God is only love and compassion and mercy, then the cross is surely meaningless, for if God is love alone, then all He needs to do when man sins is to forgive him. But the whole message is that the cross is at the centre, and without that death God, I say with reverence, cannot forgive.

So what is the trouble? And here is the answer—'God is light, and in him is no darkness at all.' And that means that He is just and righteous; it means that He is of such pure countenance that He cannot behold and look upon iniquity (Hab 1:13); it is the holiness of God that demands the cross, so without starting with holiness there is no meaning in the cross. It is not surprising that the cross has been discounted by modern theologians; it is because they have started with the love of God without His holiness. It is because they have forgotten the life of God, His holy life, that everything in Him is holy; with God love and forgiveness are not things of weakness or compromise. He can only forgive sin as He has dealt with it in His own holy manner, and that is what He did upon the cross.

Therefore it is essential to start with the holiness of God; otherwise the plan of redemption, the scheme of salvation, becomes meaningless and we can see no point or purpose in some of the central doctrines of the Christian faith. But if I start with the holiness of God I see that the incarnation must take place; the cross is absolutely essential, and the resurrection and the coming of the Holy Spirit and every other part of the great plan as well. How important it is that we should start at the right place; how vital it is that we should be led by truth and not by our own ideas.

Let me give you another answer. If we start with the holiness of God we shall find that all the false claims of fellowship with God are immediately exposed. We saw earlier how prone we are to try to have fellowship with God in false ways and that they will not last.

John is going to elaborate on that great theme. There is nothing that exposes the false so much as standing face to face with a holy God. Yes, by your own efforts you can have a kind of fellowship in your imagination with that false God whom you construct for yourself. You can practise a kind of hypnotism, but it is not fellowship with God, and in your times of need you will discover that. No, God is light, and any fellowship I may have with Him is in terms of that— it exposes the false. Not only that, it delivers me at once from attempting in a false way to try to find fellowship with Him. If I start with this conception of His holiness, then I see at once that certain things I am prone to do are ultimately going to fail.

But it saves us also from another thing; it saves us from the terrible danger of tending to blame God and to criticise Him in times of trouble and in times of need, and that is one of our greatest dangers—to misunderstand God, to argue and to question, 'Why does God do this; did I deserve this?' But if I start with the holiness of God I will never speak like that. I know at once that whatever may be happening to me is not the result of anything unworthy in God. 'God is light, and in him is no darkness at all', so that whatever may be happening to me is not in any way due to any imperfections in God; it silences me, I put my hand upon my mouth and prevent myself from speaking foolishly and whiningly.

And lastly, it is right and essential that we should start with the holiness of God because actually, in practice and as a matter of fact, it is the only way that leads to true joy. There are false joys, there is a false way of finding peace. You know those great, profound psychologists of the soul, the much maligned Puritans, used to write at great length on what they called a 'false peace'; there was nothing they were more afraid of than having a false peace with God. The most dangerous thing is for people to persuade themselves that all is right with God and then not to find Him in the moment of agony. There is such a thing as a false spirit; that is why the Bible tells us to 'try the spirits' (1 Jn 4:1), to examine ourselves, whether we are in the faith (2 Cor 13:5). There is only one way to true and lasting joy, and that is to start with the holiness of God. If I start there, I shall be delivered from every false peace, from every false joy. I shall be humbled to the dust, I shall see my true unworthiness and that

I deserve nothing at the hands of God. I shall come to the only one who can deliver me, the Lord Jesus Christ, and anything I may receive from Him is true; if I receive joy from Christ, it is a true joy, a real and lasting joy.

So you see after all John is not contradicting himself, he is not playing with us and mocking us. 'These things write we unto you, that your joy may be full.' How is my joy to be full? 'The first thing,' says John, in effect, 'is this: if you want that blessing in your life, if you want to be filled, clear out all the rubbish that is in it. If your life is to be full of joy, get rid of everything that is false; then, when it is truly emptied, it can be filled to overflowing with the true joy of the Lord in the Lord Jesus Christ.'

Thank God for the thoroughness of the gospel! Thank God for the heavenly way which starts by holding us face to face with a holy, absolute God and then driving us, leading us to the only Saviour, the Lord Jesus Christ. 'This then is the message that we have received of him and declare unto you, that God is light, and in him is no darkness at all.' We can do nothing better, every time we go on our knees to pray, than just to say that, and when we feel like rushing into our own desires and complaints, just to pause and, like the author of the epistle to the Hebrews, approach him with reverence and godly fear, 'for our God is a consuming fire.'

10

Sin

If we say that we have fellowship with him, and walk in darkness, we lie, and do not the truth: but if we walk in the light, as he is in the light, we have fellowship one with another, and the blood of Jesus Christ his Son cleanseth us from all sin. If we say that we have no sin, we deceive ourselves, and the truth is not in us. If we confess our sins, he is faithful and just to forgive us our sins, and to cleanse us from all unrighteousness. If we say that we have not sinned, we make him a liar, and his word is not in us.

1 JOHN 1:6-10

We have been looking at verse 5–'This then is the message which we have heard of him, and declare unto you, that God is light, and in him is no darkness at all', and you remember that the way John seems to look at the whole situation can be put like this: Fellowship is a position in which two people are, if you like, walking together along the road; it is a journey, a companionship. There is that key verse in the Old Testament–'Enoch walked with God' (Gen 5:22). That means he had fellowship with God, and that is a very good way of thinking of it. You see two people walking together down the road, or a husband and wife going together through life, walking through the pilgrimage; that is the idea, and the Christian is one who in that way is walking with God, journeying through this world. So obviously, when you come to consider the nature of fellowship like that, you have at least two things to do. First, you must know something about the character of the two persons who are taking part in the fellowship, and that is why John immediately begins with this very theme and there in that fifth verse he reminds us of the essential nature and character and being of God. 'If you are interested in this fellowship,' says the Apostle in effect, 'if you want to know something about it and to understand what it means; if you want it to persist and continue, then the point at which you have to start is this, the character of God. God is light, and in Him is no darkness at all; utter, absolute holiness, without blemish, without spot, without any admixture of that which is evil and sinful.'

And now in these verses John comes to the other half of the fellowship. It is important that we should know the character of God, but we must also know something about ourselves. There are two parties to this companionship; and there are certain things, according to John, that must be true on both sides before there can be a real fellowship. So here in these verses he comes to this consideration of what must be true of us if we are to enjoy that fellowship with God.

The Apostle here does not merely stop at a consideration of our character and of what must be true of us; he also deals with the limitations and the imperfections that are in us. Obviously we cannot in one study deal exhaustively with all that we are told in these verses, so we shall simply take up one particular aspect of the doctrine now and then subsequently go on to deal with the rest. But here we are confronted at once with what perhaps can be most definitely described as the biblical doctrine of sin. And immediately we come to something which causes, and has always caused, a good deal of difficulty and confusion in the minds of large numbers of people.

The doctrine of sin has never been popular. I suppose also that it is true to say that it has been even more unpopular in the last hundred years, and especially perhaps in the last fifty years, than it has ever been, and there are many people who are utterly impatient at the very mention of the word. Yet it is my whole business and purpose in expounding the Scripture to point out that the doctrine of sin is as integral a part of the biblical teaching as is the doctrine of the holiness of God. It is as true to say that man is sinful as it is to say that God is light and that in Him is no darkness at all.

This is a truth that is to be found everywhere in the Bible. Indeed, I would not hesitate to say that the doctrine of the Bible simply cannot be understood unless we accept this particular teaching, and yet people object to it. There is a kind of general objection; the average person today, without thinking about the doctrine and without examining it, just dismisses it as being soft. 'Ah,' they say, 'that old-fashioned doctrine in which the fathers delighted, with their morbidity and almost perversion! They talked of sin and preached about it, and hasn't that been part of the whole trouble? It made men live a kind of cramped and narrow life; they did not know what life and living meant. They so turned in upon themselves, and so overpainted this picture of our imperfections, that they really put fetters upon mankind.'

Indeed, the argument has been that with our new knowledge and learning, acquired especially in the last century, we have emancipated ourselves out of all this; we have got rid of this talk of sin and of all that would drag and keep us down. Having freed ourselves from the fetters of mid-Victorianism which so delighted in the doctrine of sin, we are now living this freer and much fuller and more glorious life. That has been the tendency. The feeling is that the doctrine of sin has made the whole of life miserable; it has painted it in sombre, dark colours, and all the brightness and the light has been taken out of it. And thus the Church throughout the centuries has been standing between man and his true heritage and has drawn an utterly perverted picture of life. Indeed, the modern view is that men and women who have been canonised by the Church as saints have been monstrosities!

So there is this common deep-seated objection to the whole New Testament doctrine of sin, and, of course, along with that goes the view of life which maintains that really things are not quite as bad as the Bible and the theologians in the past have made it out to be. 'So long as we do our best', people say, 'and look to God occasionally for a little help, then everything can be put right. We must not take these things too seriously; to be a Christian is to be as decent as we can be and to do good and so on, expecting a certain amount of aid from God. So we say our prayers and attend an occasional act of worship and thus we go on; we must not think of all this in those tragic terms of desperate sin and some overwhelming need of the grace of God.'

That is, in general, the modern attitude with regard to this whole subject, and this is the matter with which the Apostle John deals in these verses. He analyses this position, and he deals with it in a very radical and drastic manner. Fortunately, the subject divides itself up in a very definite way in terms of a phrase which John repeats three times. You will find the phrase in the sixth, eighth and tenth verses: 'If we say we have fellowship with him, and walk in darkness, we lie, and do not the truth.' 'If we say that we have no sin, we deceive ourselves, and the truth is not in us.' 'If we say that we have not sinned, we make him a liar, and his word is not in us.'

Now in these verses John teaches that there are three common errors with regard to this whole question of sin. And it is because we go wrong in these three main respects that so many of us, according to the Apostle, fail to enjoy and experience this amazing fellowship with God and with Jesus Christ which is offered to the Christian. So let us look at this, and again, as I do so, let me remind you of what John takes for granted as being the essence of the Christian position. It is: 'If we say that *we have fellowship with him*'—that is what we ought to say. That is what we who use the name Christian should claim; and when we say, 'I am a Christian', that is what we mean. We should not, let me emphasise again, just mean that we are a little bit better than some profligate sinner in the gutters of life, or that we are a little bit better than we once were. We should not mean that we are trying to be decent and moral, or even that we subscribe in a general and vague way to the teaching and the dogma of the Church. No. 'If we say that we have fellowship with him'—that is what we mean, says John. 'You are members of the Church,' he says to these people, 'and that is the claim you are making, that you have fellowship with God', the God whom he has just described.

This, then, is still the claim. That being so, says John, now there are certain things that must follow of necessity, and I put them like this: The first thing that comes between us and this full and glorious fellowship with God that we read of in the New Testament and in the lives of all true saints throughout the centuries is this—it is a failure to realise the nature of sin in general. This is how he puts it. Here is the claim. I say I have fellowship with God and yet I walk in darkness. Well, what of it? It is a lie, says John, and he does not apologise for being blunt and using such a strong term. If I say this and do that, it is a lie, and he goes on to say that I do not tell the truth.

So the question that confronts us is this: what is the matter with people who are in that position? John's answer is that people who are guilty of that have clearly never understood the real nature of sin. Let us take his own description of it at this point. 'If we say we have fellowship with him, and *walk in darkness*'—that is it. We are back again to this picture of companionship, a fellowship of people walking together. If we say that we are walking with him and yet in the meantime are walking in darkness, then we lie. It is not true, it is a false claim, we misinterpret ourselves to our fellow men and women and to the world, and it is all wrong.

Why is this? Well, the New Testament answer is that a person who is in that position is obviously someone who has never realised the gospel and precisely what is meant by sin. Walking in darkness, says John—or in other words, sin—is a kind of realm or atmosphere, and that is the point surely at which so many seem to go astray. They fail to realise that particular truth about sin; they will persist in thinking of it in terms of sins—particular sins and actions. But according to the Bible that is a hopelessly inadequate view of sin. Sin, according to the Bible everywhere, is a realm, a kingdom.

The Bible tells us that there are two kingdoms in this world, the kingdom of God and the kingdom of evil, the kingdom of light and the kingdom of darkness, the kingdom of holiness and the kingdom of Satan and of iniquity. There are two realms in which man can live, so that quite apart from you and me, and quite apart from our individual actions, there is such a thing as sin and evil, a realm, an attitude, an outlook, a mind. Before we were born sin was in the world. The Bible tells us that sin is the explanation of all our ills and troubles and sorrows. God made a perfect world, but then another element, sin, entered in. Man was made perfect by God, but he was tempted and fell, and the result has been that the whole world has been polluted. Thus we are reminded again of these familiar biblical phrases: 'the god of this world' (2 Cor 4:4), 'the prince of the power of the air' (Eph 2:2), that 'we wrestle not against flesh and blood, but against principalities, against powers, against the rulers of the darkness of this world, against spiritual wickedness in high places' (Eph 6:12).

There is another mighty power, a great kingdom, and, according to the Bible there is a mighty contention between these two powers, fighting for supremacy over man in this life and world. The kingdom of God and the kingdom of Satan, heaven and hell—there is a great clash between these forces. And also according to the biblical doctrine, all of us that are born into this world are born under the domination of this kingdom of darkness; and as we are by nature, we tend to live and to think in that way. The kingdom of darkness, or, if you like, 'walking in darkness', represents everything that is opposed to God, everything that is opposed to His holiness and perfection, everything that is opposed to His desires for the world and for man.

'Walking in darkness' means that you live in such a way that you rarely have any thought about God at all; and if you do think about Him, you do not think of Him as 'light [in whom] is no darkness at all'. You think of Him as some benign fatherly person who is ready to smile upon your failures and who is ready to grant you an entry into heaven at the end. That is walking in darkness—the failure to realise that the very organisation of man, the outlook of humanity, is opposed to God, that godlessness is in control and in power and that it dominates everything.

John goes on to describe this in detail in the next chapter: 'Love not the world, neither the things that are in the world. . . . For all that is in the world, the lust of the flesh, and the lust of the eyes, and the pride of life, is not of the Father, but is of the world' (1 Jn 2:15-16). That is it! 'Now,' says John at this point, 'people who have not realised all that are walking in darkness. They do not know it; they are living and thinking and acting in a realm that is the very antithesis to that which is towards God—God is light and in Him is no darkness at all.' We have seen His desires with regard to this world, but here are people who are walking utterly oblivious to all these things; they do not take any interest in them; these things do not affect their lives; they are not striving to live like that—they are walking in darkness.

And what is true of such people? Well, obviously, without any argument, they are not in fellowship with God. This is utterly impossible, for as the Apostle Paul argues in 2 Corinthians 6:14, 'What communion hath light with darkness?' You cannot mix light and dark; both are destroyed, as it were; there are certain things that are utterly incompatible, and this is one of them. Someone whose whole outlook upon life is governed by what you might call world-liness, and who thinks only in human, earthly terms of all that stands for the pride of life, such a one cannot be walking along the same road with God who is light and in whom is no darkness at all. It is impossible. So that is the first essential—that we should realise this whole doctrine about sin as a domination, as a power and as a taint in the world; for if we do not, then we cannot be in fellowship with God.

But John, you notice, goes on to say that not only must we regard it intellectually, we must also practise it—'If we say that we have fellowship with him, and walk in darkness, we lie and do not the truth.' God does what He is. God is not only light, He acts as light, and the same thing applies to man. We really show what we are by what we do; we reveal our doctrine in our practice, and those who have not realised the truth about sin, and certainly those who have a wrong idea about it all, cannot be having real fellowship and communion with God. That is the first thing.

Then the second message is in verse 8: 'If we say that we have no sin, we deceive ourselves, and the truth is not in us.' Let me put it in this way: The second failure is not to realise that our very natures are sinful. That is what John means, and this is a most important point. You see the difference? The reference here is not to acts of sin, but to the nature that produces the acts of sin. He is concerned here about the state which is both the cause and the consequence of what we do, the sinful state, which is a continuous source of influence within us.

Now there are many who are in error about this, generally because we will persist in thinking of sins rather than of a sinful nature. I am sure that the authorities are quite right when they tell us that at this point John was thinking in a particular way and manner of that heresy which was very common in the early Church—we have already referred to it—the heresy of Gnosticism. There were people who argued that if we have become Christians we have been delivered from our sinful nature and we have received a new nature; therefore, because we have received this new nature, there is no sin in us. So, if we do something that is wrong, it is not we who have sinned, the sin is merely in the flesh. Hence the heresy known as *antinomianism*, which means that as long as you are a Christian and claim you know God in Christ, it is immaterial what you do, because you do not sin, it is the flesh or body that sins.

That is the view that John is countering, but it is still fairly common, because we will persist in regarding the matter from the standpoint of action rather than from the point of view of the nature within us that produces the action; and John is very stern about this—'If we say we have no sin, we deceive ourselves, and the truth is not in us.' For someone to say in this way that he has not a sinful nature is nothing but self-deception, and here again I thank God for a word that is so honest and sharp. Are we not rather tired of the popular current writings that are for ever praising us and trying to say that all our troubles are due to somebody else or to our environment? No, says the Bible, the trouble is in you; you are not being honest with yourself.

The question that should confront us all is not simply that we have committed actions that are wrong. No, surely the most important question is, 'Why did I do it; what led me to do it; what is it in me that made me think of it and play with the suggestion?' And there is only one answer; there is something wrong within me, myself; my nature is sinful. I am driven to believe that Paul must have been right when he said, 'For I know that in me (that is, in my flesh), dwelleth no good thing' (Rom 7:18). There is an evil desire, there is something perverted in my essential being, my nature is sinful. That is why we have sinful thoughts, sinful desires, sinful imaginations. There is something in my very being as the result of the

Fall that has twisted and perverted everything. There is a kind of fountain within me that gives rise to evil and iniquity; not only do I do wrong, but my nature is sinful. I must never say I have no sin. If I do, I am deliberately deceiving myself.

But how often do we do so; how we try to rationalise our sins; how clever we are at doing it, and yet how easily we see through it when somebody else does it; how easily we can expose them and tell them they are deceivers! The human heart is desperately wicked, and those who look at themselves and face themselves know that this is the simple truth about human nature, that at the centre we are wrong. Our nature is evil and sinful, and not to admit that is self-deceit, and not only that but 'the truth is not in us'.

This again is obvious. The truth is something that always enlightens us. This comes out in Ephesians 5:13: 'Whatsoever doth make manifest is light', and our Lord made this same point when He said, 'This is the condemnation, that light is come [or has come] into the world, and men loved darkness rather than light, because their deeds were evil' (Jn 3:19). People will not come to the light because they love darkness and they know that the light will reveal the darkness and they do not want it to be revealed.

So, says John, if we say we have not sinned, it is obvious that the truth is not in us, because the truth in us is like a great flashlight flashing upon the depths of our being, and all the evil spots and darkness stand out upon the screen and we see and know it and we cannot go on saying that there is no sin in us.

And that brings us in turn to the last point in verse 10: 'If we say that we have not sinned, we make him a liar, and his word is not in us.' This is the failure to realise that we as sinners need forgiveness. It is the failure to realise the nature of sin, to grasp that our own natures are sinful and to understand that we have all actually sinned and need forgiveness.

There are certain people who seem to say, 'Yes, I believe in God and I like to have fellowship with Him, and yet, you know, I have never been conscious of my sin. I do not understand that doctrine of yours. If you were to preach it to people gathered from the streets I could understand it, but I have been brought up as a Christian, I have always tried to do good; I have never been conscious of the fact that I am a sinner, that I need repentance and that I must be converted.'

Well, says John, if that is your position, 'you make him a liar, and his word is not in you.' If we do not realise that we are sinners and need the forgiveness of God; if we do not realise that we have always needed it and that we still need it; if we think that we have always been perfect or that now we are perfect as Christians; if we do not realise that we must repent, then, says John, we are making God a liar, for the 'him' referred to is none other than God Himself. John here is just stating the whole teaching of the Bible from beginning to end.

What, then, is the teaching? Paul has summarised it perfectly for us in Romans 3; this is his verdict: 'There is none righteous, no, not one' (v 10). He says, 'Now we know that what things soever the law saith, it saith to them who are under the law: that every mouth may be stopped, and *all the world may become guilty before God*' (v 19). He goes on, 'For all have sinned, and come short of the glory of God' (v 23). The Jews, the chosen people, thought they were all right: 'Those others, the Gentiles,' they said, 'are dogs; they need it, but we do not.' But God convicts Jew and Gentile; there is none righteous; the whole world, every mouth, has been stopped. That is the doctrine of the Bible; so if we say we have not sinned, we are denying the doctrine of the Bible.

But more than that, are we not denying the very doctrine of the incarnation? Why did the Son of God come into this world of sin? He came 'to save that which was lost', to provide pardon and forgiveness of sin by the shedding of His own blood and the breaking of His own body upon the cross. If I say I have no sin, I am denying the incarnation, the death and the resurrection—I am making God a liar. Indeed, if I say I have not sinned, I am thus opposing my view of life to the whole point and purpose of the grand biblical revelation; and not only am I making God a liar, I am also again proving that His word is not in me, because the word of God always convicts us; it makes us see the necessity of the cross and the atonement and all the wondrous provision that God has made.

Let me sum it up like this: Not to be right about sin, therefore, leads to these results. It means that we are still walking in darkness, that our whole attitude is a lie. If I say I am a Christian and the world knows that I am a Christian and I continue to walk in darkness, I am a liar, I am pretending to be something I am not, I am lying to other people. But, next, I am lying to myself and deceiving myself. Furthermore, I make God a liar, and ultimately I regard as absolutely unnecessary this amazing thing that God has done in Christ. I am laughing in the face of eternal love, which sent His only begotten Son into the world for our rescue and for our redemption. And is it not perfectly obvious, without any need of pressure or of argument, that if I am in that position I have no fellowship with God, for 'God is light, and in him is no darkness at all.' A lie cannot live in the presence of God; it is an utter contradiction of everything that God is, and it just means that I am not a Christian at all.

The doctrine of sin is essential, and unless I realise I am a sinner and must repent, and if my only hope is not in Christ and His death for me on the cross and His resurrection for my justification, I not only have no fellowship with God, but I am dwelling still in utter darkness. Oh yes, to have fellowship with God we must not only be clear about the nature of God, we must be equally clear about ourselves and our own nature.

But, thank God, the Apostle does not leave us at that. Having convicted us of our sin, in the self-same verse he goes on to tell us of the glorious provision—'If we walk in the light as he is in the light, we have fellowship with one another, and the blood of Jesus Christ his Son cleanseth us from all sin. If we confess our sins, he is faithful and just to forgive us our sins, and to cleanse us from all unrighteousness.'

11

Walking in the Light

If we say that we have fellowship with him, and walk in darkness, we lie, and do not the truth: but if we walk in the light, as he is in the light, we have fellowship one with another, and the blood of Jesus Christ his Son cleanseth us from all sin. If we say that we have no sin, we deceive ourselves, and the truth is not in us. If we confess our sins, he is faithful and just to forgive us our sins, and to cleanse us from all unrighteousness. If we say that we have not sinned, we make him a liar, and his word is not in us.

1 JOHN 1:6-10

John has shown that we must be perfectly clear about certain conditions that must of necessity be observed if we truly are to enjoy fellowship with God. He begins with the character and the being of God Himself; then he shows that we must be equally clear about ourselves. So we have considered what may be called the negative aspect of this—our sinfulness—and now we come to what we may call the positive side of the matter.

You notice that there are certain contrasts which he applies—'If we say that we have fellowship with him, and walk in darkness, we lie, and do not the truth: but if we walk in the light, as he is in the light, we have fellowship one with another, and the blood of Jesus Christ his Son cleanseth us from all sin. If we say that we have no sin, we deceive ourselves, and the truth is not in us'—then, 'If we confess our sins, he is faithful and just to forgive us our sins, and to cleanse us from all unrighteousness.' So we are looking now particularly at verses 7 and 9 where he puts all his emphasis on what we have to do in a positive sense. We must see clearly what the positive conditions are which we must fulfil in order to make this fellowship possible, and in order that it may continue.

Here, again, is a statement which must once more be subdivided into two parts. In order to make this fellowship active we have certain things to do and God must do certain things to us: 'If we walk in the light, as he is in the light, we have fellowship one with another'—that is what we do; 'and the blood of Jesus Christ his Son cleanseth us from all sin'—that is what He does. 'If we confess our sins'—that again is our part; then, 'He is faithful and just to forgive us our sins, and to cleanse us from all unrighteousness.' So it is quite inevitable in the matter of fellowship like this that though in a logical sense we persist in dividing up the aspect of fellowship into the two sides—Godward and manward—they are constantly intermixed and intermingled, because it is a sharing together, it is an interaction of the one upon the other.

In other words, fellowship is never mechanical, but always something organic and vital. Yet, of course, if we would understand it truly, for the sake of clarity of thought we are allowed to analyse it in the way we are doing, but we must remember that organic nature. To use an illustration: what we are doing is what the musicians do when they analyse a piece of music like a sonata or a symphony. It is right to say that it is composed of various parts and you can make an analysis of it, but if you are truly to appreciate it you must always remember it is a whole and you must take it as such. You cannot stop at an analysis, nor can you leave it at these various bits and portions; they are there, but they are parts of the whole.

Or to take another illustration: the human body consists of separate parts, and while, of course, you can think of the parts as distinct from the body—you recognise the hand, for example, and the fingers—yet the hand has no meaning in and of itself. So in order to get a good conception of the body it is right to study anatomy and physiology—to divide up the body into various parts, and to study how they all work. But we must never forget that the body is organically a whole; it is an essential, vital unit.

Now that is always essential also in taking any passage of Scripture, but it seems to be particularly true of this first epistle of John with his strange and unusual type of mind. You remember that we described his method of thought as being a spiral one; the steps and stages are not as clear on the surface as they are, say, in the writings of Paul, so in considering his teaching it is very important to bear these two aspects in mind.

Here, then, again is something which is absolutely vital and essential if we are to enjoy true fellowship with God, and first we must consider what we must do with regard to this positive aspect of fellowship. Then we shall consider what God does at this particular point in maintaining the reality of fellowship. But before we begin to do this, let me make some preliminary introductory remarks.

This paragraph is one that notoriously has figured a great deal in theological and religious thought and discussion. There is no passage, perhaps, that is quoted so frequently, when people are concerned about the whole problem and question of sanctification, as this particular one, and that constitutes, in a sense, a danger and adds to our difficulties.

The danger always in interpreting a passage of Scripture like this is that instead of going to Scripture itself and considering what it has to say, we tend to go to it with our ready-made theory and then go on to interpret the statement in the light of that theory and idea. You are familiar with what I mean. What you find is this verse quoted: 'The blood of Jesus Christ his Son cleanseth us from all sin'; and then this other verse: 'He is faithful and just to forgive us our sins, and to cleanse us from all unrighteousness.' Then how often with reference to holiness and sanctification is this verse used: 'walk in the light, as he is in the light.' A great deal is heard about all these verses—they are always popular in this connection—'walking in the light'; 'confessing our sins'; 'the blood of Jesus Christ cleanseth us' and 'he is faithful and just.'

Now it is difficult not to think of these verses in the light of some particular theory of sanctification which we may happen to hold, because the history of this doctrine shows very clearly that we seem to be particularly prone when dealing with it to accept theories based often upon one statement in Scripture and that often taken out of its context. So there is nothing more important in dealing with these verses than that we really should in the first instance make a very special effort to rid our minds of these prejudices and pre-conceived ideas and theories and to consider the statement of Scripture especially in its own particular context.

What adds to our problem, in a sense, is the kind of language of which the Apostle was so fond. Anybody who has ever studied John's Gospel, his epistles and the book of the Revelation will know that John's style is rather characterised by his fondness for certain controlling ideas. He is fond of the ideas of light and of life. He plays with them, and you will find them running constantly right through everything he has ever written; and one of the greatest dangers is that we tend to forget that. John thought pictorially, and the danger is to literalise something which he intended to be just a picture. The result is that you find that most theories with regard to perfectionism tend to base themselves on the writings of John and especially on this first epistle. But I hope to be able to show you that most people have gone astray because they will not recognise his pictures as pictures, and will insist upon materialising them. And thereby they inevitably find themselves teaching a doctrine of perfection in some shape or form.

Those, then, are the preliminary considerations. So coming to the actual statement, what is it that we have to do? Well, according to John, there are two main things: first, we must walk in the light as He is in the light.

Now here I think we come across an illustration of what I have just been saying. John is fond of the phrase, 'walking in the light'; how often it occurs in the Gospel and here it is again. Is it not obvious on the very surface that if you take this in an absolute literal sense it can mean only one thing, and that is absolute perfection. If to walk in the light as God is in the light is taken strictly literally, as it is expressed here, there is only one deduction to draw: as Christians our only hope of forgiveness and therefore of being

Christian at all is that we should be absolutely perfect as God Himself is perfect.

But clearly that is impossible! Which of us is perfect, which of us is without sin? 'If we say that we have no sin, we deceive ourselves, and the truth is not in us'; we cannot, therefore, be absolutely perfect. So immediately we find that this phrase of walking in the light as God is in the light must be interpreted in terms of the way in which he customarily employs this picture. And the key to that is to be found in the phrase we have already considered in the previous verse in which we read about walking in darkness— 'If we say we have fellowship with him, and walk in darkness, we lie and do not the truth.'

Now we saw that walking in darkness meant living in the realm of darkness, being controlled by the ideas of the world and of sin, belonging to a kingdom, the kingdom of darkness, the kingdom of Satan, the kingdom of this world, the kingdom that is rebellious against the kingdom of God. In other words, the people who walk in darkness are not those who, as it were, are constantly committing some foul sin. They may be highly respectable—indeed, they may be very moral—but they are walking in darkness because they are outside the light of the gospel of our Lord and Saviour Jesus Christ; it is a realm to which people belong; it is an outlook upon life in general.

So when we come to this verse about 'walking in the light', we interpret it as just the antithesis and the exact opposite of 'walking in darkness'. Therefore it does not mean that I claim absolute perfection; but it does mean that I claim that I now belong to a different realm, to the kingdom of light and to the kingdom of God. In that kingdom, alas, I may be most unworthy; but though unworthy, I am in it and I belong to it and I am walking in the realm of light. God is the God of that kingdom, and God is in that kingdom as the King, as the Lord.

So that to 'walk in the light as he is in the light' means that, to use the language of the Apostle Paul in writing to the Colossians, I have been translated from the kingdom of darkness into 'the kingdom of his dear son' (Col 1:13). The Apostle Peter in his first epistle is really expressing the same doctrine when he says, 'Ye are a chosen generation, a royal priesthood, a holy nation, a peculiar people; that ye should show forth the praises of him who hath called you out of darkness into his marvellous light' (1 Pet 2:9). That is it! It is the kingdom to which we belong.

I emphasise this because you will find that certain people with their particular theory of holiness and sanctification are always teaching that the only people who walk in the light are certain very special Christians. Whereas what John is saying is that every Christian of necessity is one who is walking in the light. The non-Christian is the one who is walking in darkness; all Christians, however feeble, unworthy and faltering, are people who are walking in the light; otherwise they are not Christians at all and none of the remarks of the Apostle in any way apply to them.

That is the first point, which we must grasp very clearly. What does it mean in practice? It surely means two things most of all. Firstly, we cannot claim that we are walking in the light unless we have repented. In other words, we are people who have had our eyes opened to the whole of that doctrine of sin that we were considering together earlier. How do I know I am walking in the light? This is one of the best answers: we have come to realise that we were 'born in sin and shapen in iniquity'; that by nature, by birth, 'we are all the children of wrath'. We have come to realise that we were slaves, born under the dominion of sin and of Satan; that we were living in the realm of darkness; that our very nature was sinful and that we have sinned. We have got this new view of sin; we have seen that, and, of course, having seen it, we have bemoaned the fact. We regret it; we have known what it is to feel a godly sorrow because of it. Those who repent are those who have so seen themselves that they have become alarmed about themselves. They know what it is to say, 'O wretched man that I am! who shall deliver me from the body of this death?' (Rom 7:24). This is essential to being a Christian, for no one is a Christian, no one can be walking in the light, who has not seen it.

But you notice it does not stop at that—that is only a kind of initial step. Man, like the prodigal of old, becoming aware of his situation, realises his desperate problem and says, 'I will arise and go to my Father', and he gets up and goes to him; he changes his whole realm and position. The Christian must do this, so it includes positive living; it does not stop at repentance and an acknowledgement and awareness of sin. It means a positive endeavour to live in a manner worthy of one who has been translated into the kingdom of God's dear Son.

What it means, therefore, is that men and women who walk in the light are people who are seeking God. They desire to know God better; they are concerned about the glory and honour of God; they are anxious to please God. They realise that for very many years they have been living in a realm which is antagonistic to God, and their whole idea is to be as different as they can. That is walking in the light, living to the glory and honour of God. God is their Master; they seek righteousness and are concerned about being holy. Now that, I suggest to you, is the teaching of the Apostle at this point.

Let me try to emphasise this as a doctrine. I think you will agree with me that there is, perhaps, no doctrine that has been so frequently misunderstood as this doctrine of what is meant by 'walking in the light'. There have been two misconceptions. The first we have dealt with under the heading of mysticism and monasticism. There are people who, having awakened to the fact that they are sinners and are in the realm of darkness, say, 'Now what we have to do is to walk in the light; how is that to be done?' And their answer is, 'There is only one thing to do; we must segregate ourselves from the world, we must go right out of it. To walk in the light means that we must make this a whole-time job; we must seek God directly by the mystical road, or we must go right away and occupy ourselves fully with certain religious works and thereby we will be enabled to walk in the light.' Read the story of monasticism and mysticism and you will find it was this idea of walking in the light that was at the back of it; that was the idea that led men to take up this vocation of the holy and godly life. That is one error.

The other error is at the other extreme. It is the failure to see the importance of conduct and of behaviour. Let me put this carefully. This is perhaps the besetting danger of those of us who are Protestants and who are most evangelical. We say that the one thing we must avoid is a belief in justification by works, the tendency to say that it is a matter of living a good life that makes us Christians, that it is because we walk in the light that we are Christians. We must not rely upon our works, we say; that is the whole error of Catholicism in its various forms. We say that nothing matters but that we believe on the Lord Jesus Christ and in His death for us and our sin. We are justified by faith only, without deeds.

Yes, but consider also what the Apostle Paul says in 1 Corinthians 6. This is the Apostle of faith, remember, this is the man above all men who preached this doctrine of justification by faith only, and this is what he says: 'Be not deceived; neither fornicators, nor idolaters, nor adulterers, nor effeminate, nor abusers of themselves with mankind, nor thieves, nor covetous, nor drunkards, nor revilers, nor extortioners, shall inherit the kingdom of God' (vs 9-10). 'How do you reconcile these things?' asks someone. Surely the only way to reconcile them is this—and this, it seems to me, is the very thing the Apostle John was anxious to teach at this point. There is only one proof of the fact that I have really seen the truth; there is only one ultimate proof of the fact that I have faith, that my eyes have been opened to the gospel and its message, and it is this: that having seen myself as a condemned sinner, I have forsaken sin, I have repented, and I am striving with all my might and main to 'walk in the light as he is in the light'.

In other words, John is testing our Christian profession. What John is really saying, in effect, is, 'It is no use your saying, "I believe", and then living as if you believed nothing. It is no use saying, "I believe I am such a sinner and that nothing but the death of Christ can save me", and then continuing to live that kind of life. It is impossible,' says John; 'we give a proof of our repentance by the life which we live.' There is no value in a supposed faith that does not lead to action. There is no contradiction between John and Paul; they are both saying the same thing.

So, there are two sides; both are essential, and faith and works are inseparable. That is the way to test the difference between intellectual assent and true faith. There are men and women who accept the Christian teaching as a journal of philosophy, but they do nothing about it. As I understand the New Testament, they are not Christians, they are not walking in the light. A person's acts prove what faith they have; walking in the light means repentance and turning from sin to holiness of life; these are the ultimate proofs of the genuineness of a true Christian profession.

So that is the first thing that John emphasises—that we must walk in the light as He is in the light—and the important declaration therefore which is made is that everyone who is truly Christian is walking in the realm of light and not in the realm of darkness. Let me add once more, I do not say that they are perfect. They may be imperfect, they may be guilty of sin, but thank God they can say, 'I am not like those people in the world; I am not like those men and women who do not believe in Christ. I am essentially different, though in many respects I am guilty of the same things as they are.' You see, therefore, the utter error of those who are outside Christ. They say, 'What is the use of being a Christian? Look at your Christians!' As if that proved it! No. What makes people Christians is the realm in which they are walking; it is the kingdom to which they belong.

The second matter, of course, is confession of sin, and this again is essential. 'If we confess our sins, he is faithful and just to forgive . . . '. Now this, too, is essential, so let me tabulate what seems to be the argument in the Apostle's mind. Why does a refusal on my part to confess my sins break and interrupt fellowship? It does so for these reasons. The light always reveals the hidden things of darkness; so if I refuse to face my sin, it means first of all that I am avoiding the light. I am concealing and refusing to face something, and that breaks fellowship with God, because God is light. Or, to put it another way, it means that I am resisting the Holy Spirit, for it is the work of the Spirit to bring my hidden sins to light, to convict me of that and to lead me to forsake them.

It also means that I am refusing to be honest with myself; and if I am not honest with myself, how can I be honest with God? The person who is dishonest is not in relationship and cannot enjoy fellowship; the man who is dishonest cuts himself off automatically from his partner or friend. If a man is not true to himself, as Shakespeare put it, then he is false to every man; but if you are true, you cannot be false to anyone.

Lastly, not facing my sins means that I dislike the light, and is this not true of us? We dislike the light of the gospel; we want to be told about the love of God, but we dislike the light, and if that is so, how can we walk with God who is light?

Confession is essential. It means that we must remain open to the work of the light, we must let it search us, we must pull down the defences, and we must come to the Word honestly.

Then secondly, we must recognise our sins in particular. This is a painful process; to confess my sins does not just mean that I say in general, 'Well, I am a sinner—I have never claimed to be a saint.' No, rather it comes to the details. I must confess my particular sins, I must name them one by one; it means that I must not gloss over them, I must not attempt to deny them. I must confess them, I must look at them. There must be no attempt to dismiss them as quickly as possible. Confession means facing them, not trying to balance up the sins I have committed and the good deeds I have done. No, I must let the light so search me that I feel miserable and wretched— this honest facing of the things I have done and of what I am; it means that I must confess it to God in words.

Surely it is unnecessary that I should emphasise here that not for one second at this point does John mention my confessing my sins to anybody else. He is not concerned about anybody else; he is concerned about fellowship with God, my walking with God; and what he tells me is that having confessed my sin and confessed it to myself, I confess it to God. 'If we confess our sins, he is faithful and just to forgive us our sins, and to cleanse us from all unrighteousness.'

How often has this verse of John's been used to teach one of the pet theories of holiness and sanctification—that unless you make open confession of your sins to all and sundry at all times you cannot be walking in the light. But John does not say that. He is concerned about my fellowship with God, my walk with God. I am prepared to agree that there are certain conditions and circumstances in which I have to confess my sin to another. If I have sinned against another person, if there are some particular circumstances where another person is involved, I have to do that. But neither here nor anywhere else in Scripture will you find any teaching that tells you you are not walking in the light unless you are all the time exposing all your sins to everybody. No, we must confess our sins to God; we must acknowledge them to Him, mentioning them to Him in detail, baring them, laying them open before Him as David did in Psalm 32, and then, and then only, are we assured of this great and glorious blessing which He is ready to give us.

Yet there is an emphasis upon the human side in this matter. I must walk in the light, and as I see and recognise my sins, as I am convicted of my sins, as I walk with God, as the holiness and the light of His nature reveals them to me, I confess them. I do not care to evade or avoid them; I acknowledge and admit them to Him, and having done that, my side of the fellowship is fulfilled and the glory of the gospel is that if I do that— and how simple it is—then God will do something for me which He alone can do. He will give me joy unspeakable and full of glory!

12

The Blood of Jesus Christ

If we say that we have fellowship with him, and walk in darkness, we lie, and do not the truth: but if we walk in the light, as he is in the light, we have fellowship one with another, and the blood of Jesus Christ his Son cleanseth us from all sin. If we say that we have no sin, we deceive ourselves, and the truth is not in us. If we confess our sins, he is faithful and just to forgive us our sins, and to cleanse us from all unrighteousness. If we say that we have not sinned, we make him a liar, and his word is not in us.

1 JOHN 1:6-10

We have seen that what we must do if our fellowship with God is to continue can be put like this: We must walk in the light, and we must confess and acknowledge our sins. It is no use our talking about fellowship with God if we walk in the realm of darkness; no, we must walk in the light and we must repent, believe on the Lord Jesus Christ, and follow Him. And in addition to that, we must confess and acknowledge our sins. But that in and of itself is not sufficient, because we must recognise at once that if we are walking with God and having fellowship with Him, it follows of necessity that we shall be more conscious than ever of our sinfulness and our unworthiness; and that is the great problem always with regard to this whole matter of fellowship with God.

Our first tendency, as we have seen, foolishly and ignorantly, is to think that as we are we have that fellowship with God; but the moment we are convicted of sin we are soon delivered from that. Then the next stage is the one in which we begin to feel hopeless because we are so conscious of our sin and of the holiness of God that we begin to say at once, 'Surely fellowship with God is a sheer and utter impossibility.' Light, we have said, is something that exposes the hidden things of darkness; light always reveals things of which we were unconscious. Light in a room will do that; it will reveal dust and various other things; light on a dark road in the country reveals all sorts of things. It is the character of light to reveal the hidden things of darkness, and this is supremely true of walking with God. When we walk with God and when His Word dwells within us, of necessity we are convicted of sin; everything that is wrong, unworthy and sinful in us is at once brought to the surface.

To use an illustration, we are aware of this very principle when we come into contact with particularly godly and saintly men or women. We cannot be in the presence of such people without at once being conscious of all our defects and all our sins and imperfections. It is not that these godly people draw attention to them in words, nor do they make an analysis of us or point a finger at us; but the effect of saintliness upon us is at once to bring all those things to the surface and we are terribly conscious of them. Well, multiply that by infinity and there you find yourself in the presence of God. The presence of God at once convicts of sin.

In other words, as we have fellowship with God and as we walk with Him in the light, we all experience what the Apostle Peter experienced during one of the first contacts he had with our Lord when our Lord worked a miracle. They had been unable to catch any fish; they had tried, but they had failed, and our Lord sent them back again to the very self-same place and there they had a great haul of fish, and you remember the effect that that had upon Peter. Peter, seeing and realising something of our Lord's Godhead and glory, said, 'Depart from me; for I am a sinful man, O Lord' (Lk 5:8). That is the effect of realising something of the glory of the Son of God incarnate on earth—'Depart from me, O Lord, I am not fit to be in Your presence; I am so conscious of my sin.'

That is what happens when we are truly in the presence of God. So at once the question arises, What can we do? We are trying to walk in the light, we are doing our utmost, we are confessing our sins, but that in and of itself seems to break the fellowship and make it impossible, for our conscience condemns us and we feel we cannot dwell in such a glorious light. And it is in order to answer that question that we must return again to verses 7 and 9. In other words, I want now to emphasise the other side, that which I have already described as the godward side, or the godward aspect. 'If we walk in the light, as he is in the light, we have fellowship one with another, *and the blood of Jesus Christ his Son cleanseth us from all sin.*' 'If we confess our sins, *he is faithful and just to forgive us our sins, and to cleanse us from all unrighteousness.*' And those are the two phrases that we must consider now.

We are confronting here, as we have seen, two statements that have often led to a great deal of discussion and controversy; they are great and glorious phrases, and yet I want to try to show you that they are very often misunderstood and misinterpreted, so that if we are to derive their full benefit and value we must try to discover the meaning that the Apostle was anxious to convey to those people to whom he wrote the letter. There are two main principles here. Firstly, what God has provided to meet our need; and the second is the assurance which we should have in view of God's provision.

What has God provided for us in this matter of fellowship with Him as we become conscious of our sin? The answer is: 'The blood of Jesus Christ his Son cleanseth us from all sin.' 'He is faithful and just to forgive us our sins, and to cleanse us from all unrighteousness.' Yes, but the question is, what do those phrases mean; what is John exactly teaching at that point? Well, in order to concentrate our attention upon it, let me put the question—is John's teaching here with regard to justification only, or does it go on to include sanctification at the same time?

Now we can observe an interesting thing at this point. John does not use the terms justification and sanctification; they are

Paul's great words, but, of course, John teaches exactly the same doctrine. Furthermore, I think that much of the trouble with regard to these matters has arisen because people will not see that fact. John, in his own pictorial way, is teaching precisely the same truth as the Apostle Paul teaches in his more logical and legal manner by means of his terms justification and sanctification, righteousness and redemption, and so on. So the best way in which to answer our question is to define the two terms.

What, then, is meant by justification? Justification is the New Testament term which represents our standing in the presence of God. Justification means not only the forgiveness of our sins, but also that our sins have been dealt with and have been removed from us. Justification states that God regards us as righteous, as if we had not sinned. In other words, it is a stronger term than forgiveness; we may be forgiven and yet our sins remain upon us. But what God does for us in justification is to remove the guilt altogether, to remove the sin. It is not only that He does not punish us for it, but that He looks upon us as righteous, as if we had not sinned; that sin has been removed.

Sanctification, on the other hand, is that condition in which the sin principle is being dealt with. Justification does not deal with the sin principle which is within us; it deals with the sins that we have committed. But after our sins have been forgiven and sin and guilt have been removed from us, the sin principle will remain within us, and what the New Testament means by this doctrine of sanctification is the process whereby the very principle and the activity of sin within us is being taken out of us and removed. Furthermore, we are assured that ultimately that will be completed, and we shall therefore be finally delivered not only from the guilt of sin but also from the power of sin and even from the pollution of sin. So the point to bear in mind is that the difference between justification and sanctification is the difference between dealing with the sins that we have committed and their effect upon us, and dealing with the principle of sin that resides within us.

Now the great question here is which of these two the Apostle John is dealing with in these phrases. This is not just a purely theoretical or academic point. No, the importance of this question arises in this way. I think I can say quite honestly as a pastor and as one who deals with the souls of men and women privately and individually, as well as preaching from a Christian pulpit, that more men and women have come to speak to me on this particular question than on any other. I know of many Christian people who are unhappy or troubled and who have found themselves in great difficulty because of this confusion between justification and sanctification. I do not want to exaggerate this, but I have even discovered many people who have literally been on the verge of a breakdown because of confusion on this point.

There are those who seem to think that the New Testament promises us, as Christians in this life and world, a life which is absolutely free from sin and devoid of any struggle whatsoever. And because they cannot say that they have perfect peace within and that there is no struggle in their life, they begin to feel they are not Christians. Then they begin to fear, and you see them heading for a very bad psychological breakdown. It is, therefore, of vital importance that we should be clear about it. In addition, of course, we can never understand too much of the gracious doctrine of the New Testament.

So, is this justification or sanctification? Let us approach it in this way. What in the New Testament is the meaning of the phrase 'the blood of the Lord Jesus Christ' or 'the blood of Jesus'? What does it refer to? Does verse 7 mean that the blood of the Lord Jesus Christ is cleansing the sin principle right out of me, that it is sanctifying me and that I am being literally purged from sin as a power until I shall be absolutely free from it? Is that what the blood of Christ does? I suggest to you that if you examine every single reference to this phrase in the new Testament you will find that it invariably refers to the death of our Lord—for example, 'In whom we have redemption through his blood, the forgiveness of sins' (Eph 1:7). Take any verse you like and you will find that invariably the blood of Jesus Christ is a reference to the blood shed upon the cross, to his death upon the cross and nothing more.

But it is just there, I think, that confusion has entered. It is not for me to criticise a great teacher and expositor like Bishop Westcott, but there can be no doubt at all that he has been mainly responsible for this confusion. In his commentary on this epistle of John, he taught that the blood represents the life. He quotes the Old Testament, where we are told that the life of the flesh is in the blood (Lev 17:11); so he says that really the effect of the shedding of blood is not so much death as the releasing of life. Therefore, he interprets the blood of Jesus Christ as the life of Jesus Christ—not His death but His life, and what we have here, therefore, he would have us believe, is that the life of Jesus Christ, the life that is in the blood, or the blood that represents the life, is cleansing us and delivering us from the power and the principle of sin that is within us and is responsible for so much.

But in all these passages referring to the blood you will find that every single time, without exception, it clearly refers to death and not to life. The object of Jesus Christ upon the cross was not simply to 'release the life principle'; it was rather to fulfil the law of God which has said that the punishment of sin is death—'the wages of sin is death' (Rom 6:23)—not the releasing of life, but the taking of life, the shedding forth of the life blood. The Apostle Paul says in Romans 5:10: 'If, when we were enemies, we were reconciled to God by the death of his Son'—the blood was shed in that death, and that is the effect—'much more, being reconciled, we shall be saved by his life.' So that surely what the Apostle is referring to here is the death of Jesus Christ, not His life.

That leads us, then, to the second question. What does the death of Jesus Christ achieve? What, according to the New Testament, is the function of the death of our Lord upon the cross, and what has resulted from it? And again I suggest to you that the answer is invariably this: Our Lord's death is that which has purchased our pardon; the death is concerned about reconciliation, about justification, about remission of sins. In other words, I am suggesting that the death of our Lord never goes beyond that.

Take again that great statement of Paul in Romans 5:10 which I have just quoted and you will see the distinction. The death of Christ deals with the guilt of sin, the pollution of sin and its tarnishing effect; sanctification and our perfection is the work of the life of Christ, the work of the risen Christ who has sent the Holy Spirit into us and upon us. The work of sanctification is surely the work of the Holy Spirit who has been given to us as the gift of God by the risen Christ. The death is concerned about the guilt of sin; the life is concerned with the power of sin and our sanctification; and therefore it seems to me that there is nothing which is worse confounded than to say that the blood of Jesus Christ has any reference whatsoever to our sanctification.

It is important we should bear that in mind at this particular point. What John is interested in is fellowship with and a possibility of walking with God. He is not interested in our sinful natures as such, but in the guilt of sin and the tarnishing which sin produces and which interrupts the fellowship. What he is anxious to show us is that though we are guilty of sins, and though we fall into sin, we can still have fellowship with God.

Let us be quite clear about this. The Bible does not teach us anywhere that fellowship with God is made impossible because sin still remains in us; if that were true no man who has ever lived would ever have fellowship with God. For if to have fellowship with God, we must be absolutely perfect and the very sin principle must have been removed, then not one of us has had fellowship with God, for we are aware of sin within ourselves. That is not what John is concerned about. He is concerned about walking with God, and what he says is that though the sin principle remains in us, though we have sinned, we can still have fellowship with God.

'Yes,' says someone, 'but what about the sins I have committed and their polluting and tarnishing effects?' 'Ah,' says John, 'the blood of Jesus Christ cleanses the very guilt and pollution and tarnishing effect and therefore you can continue in the fellowship.' Now there, I suggest to you, is the doctrine of the Apostle at this point. Let no one misunderstand me—I am not stating that sanctification does not matter. Sanctification is of supreme importance, but where sanctification comes in is this: your effort to walk in the light is part of your sanctification, and so is your confessing your sins and recognising them.

John has a great deal to say about sanctification in this epistle. He tells us to love the brethren; he tells us to be kind and loving; he tells us not to live for the things of this world—that is sanctification. But the blood of Jesus Christ has no reference to sanctification;

it is, rather, something that has reference to our justification. The question before us is just this question of finding ourselves sinful and then feeling we cannot have fellowship with God. We think we are unworthy of this fellowship, so what can we do about it? And this is John's answer to us in this glorious message.

So if that is the doctrine, then there are certain things that follow immediately, to which we must pay attention. There are certain phrases that one often hears being used in this connection which seem to me to be quite unscriptural. The Christian is not a man or woman who ought to be walking in the light but who so often is walking in darkness. The Christian is one who, by definition here, is always walking in the light even though he falls into sin. By falling into sin you do not return to walking in darkness. The Christian is not a Christian at all unless he is walking in the light.

Let me put it in this way. There are some people who seem to speak in such as way as to give the impression that one moment you are in the kingdom of God and the next moment you are in the kingdom of Satan. But the New Testament does not say that. Christians do not spend their lives walking in and out of the kingdom of God; we are all by nature in the kingdom of darkness, and by becoming Christians we are translated, put into, the kingdom of God. Let me say this, and it is a daring statement in a sense, yet it is scriptural: if I fall into sin I am still in the kingdom of God. I am not walking in darkness because I have sinned; I am still in the realm of light and in the kingdom of God even though I have sinned—the shed blood of Jesus Christ put me there. And it is this shed blood of Christ that still delivers me from the guilt of my sins in the kingdom of God.

Let me also put it like this—you sometimes hear people, in the light of this word, saying something to this effect: 'You know, we have to keep going back to Calvary'; and they draw this picture of the Christian life as a journey. You start at Calvary, and you walk in the fellowship, then you sin, and you have to go back to Calvary. No, you do not go back; in a sense Calvary is always accompanying you. You do not go back in your Christian life; if you fall into sin, you confess it and go on. It is the blood of Jesus Christ that cleanses, and Calvary is something that accompanies us in the grace and mercy of God. It is exactly like the picture which the Apostle Paul draws in 1 Corinthians 10:4, when he talks about the rock that followed the ancient people in the wilderness. That rock was Christ, he says.

Let me take just one other phrase. You have people using this self-same text and saying something like, 'Ah, yes, you must take your sin and put it under the blood.' They talk as if they are being highly scriptural, but actually they are misinterpreting the phrase. You do not find this misinterpretation in Scripture. Surely what our text teaches us is that when we sin we must confess it. We acknowledge it before God, and in His infinite mercy He will put the blood upon it. It is God who applies the blood; He is faithful and just to forgive us our sins. It is the blood of Jesus Christ that cleanses us from the guilt of sin; God has made the provision, and He applies it. We are called upon to walk in the light and to confess our sins, and as we do so He will bring to bear upon our confessed sin the provision He made on Calvary in the death of His only begotten Son. We are delivered from that guilt and pollution and from that tarnishing effect and we are conscious that the fellowship is restored and we can continue. In other words, I suggest to you that sanctification does not enter into this phrase at all, that the whole time the Apostle is concerned about justification, and then the rest of the epistle in a sense is just an elaboration of the great doctrine of sanctification.

Let me, finally, emphasise the assurance which the Christian has in the light of this wonderful provision. This is one of the most comforting statements in the Holy Scriptures. Here am I anxious to have fellowship with God and to walk with Him in the light, but I find myself sinning. Then the devil comes and says, 'You are no Christian; you cannot walk with Him; look at your sin and your guilt!'—and one feels hopeless. But here is the glorious answer to that, and this is our assurance—'The blood of Jesus Christ cleanses us'—it goes on doing so and will continue to do it—'from all sin'. 'He is faithful and just to forgive us our sins, and to cleanse us from all unrighteousness.'

How can I hope to have this forgiveness of my sins? The

answer is that the blood of the Son of God cleanses me from it. Look at David in Psalm 51, conscious of pollution and of the need of cleansing. 'This pollution, this tarnished effect of sin,' he cries, 'what can take it from me? Hyssop is not enough; the blood of bulls and of goats is not enough.' No, I need something that can cleanse me and give me assurance, and this is what I am told: it is the blood of Jesus Christ His Son, and I can trust this. Or as the Apostle Peter puts it in his first epistle, where he reminds us that we should be perfect and clear in our minds that we have been delivered from our sinfulness and from our vain conversation inherited by tradition from our fathers, not 'with corruptible things, as silver and gold . . . but with the precious blood of Christ, as of a lamb without blemish and without spot' (1 Pet 1:18-19). All the solutions of the world are insufficient to get rid of the stain of my sins, but here is the blood of the Son of God, spotless, blameless, and I feel that this is powerful.

> *There is power, power, wonder-working power*
> *In the precious blood of the Lamb.*

> *His blood can make the foulest clean,*
> *His blood availed for me.*
>
> Charles Wesley

That is our comfort and consolation.

But in addition, 'He is faithful and just to forgive us our sins, and to cleanse us from all unrighteousness.' What does this mean? Well, says John, if you want further comfort and assurance, here it is—it is the very character of God Himself. God has promised that in Christ He has provided the way. He promised it in the old dispensation; He gave us types and shadows, all the ceremonies of the levitical priesthood. But, God said, I am going to provide a perfect sacrifice, and when He comes, sin will be entirely forgiven. And God is faithful; all He has promised has been perfectly fulfilled. He has promised that if we confess our sins, if we look to His Son dying upon that cross, He will forgive us freely. Therefore have no doubts, says John; rely upon the faithfulness of God to His own word and promises.

But even stronger than that, John tells us that God is just, and this is John's way of putting what Paul has said in Romans 3:25. Paul puts it like this: The problem of sin to God, if I may put it with reverence, is, how can He forgive sin and still remain a holy and just God? The answer is in the cross of Christ. He has set Him forth 'to be a propitiation for our sins', and the result is that in the light of the death of Christ upon the cross, God can be 'just and the justifier' (v 26) of the ungodly. The cross of Christ justifies God; he remains holy because He has punished sin in the death, the shed blood, of His Son.

So as I am aware of my sinfulness and my unworthiness and my unrighteousness, I look to the blood of Jesus Christ, and I see there the forgiveness of God. I see the justice of God; I know that there God has forgiven and still forgives and will forgive. It is not that I am to make merchandise of the blood of Christ; not that I am to regard the blood of Christ as a cheap thing which allows me to continue in sin that grace may abound. No, it is that I can have this confidence that the death of Christ upon the cross is the propitiation for my sins—indeed, for the sins of the whole world—and that all my sins have been dealt with and are covered, are removed and banished there in Him.

Knowing thus the faithfulness and justice of God and the power of the blood of Christ to deliver me and to cleanse me from the guilt and stain of my sins, I can with confidence go forward, knowing that all is clear, my conscience has been cleansed, and I can continue to walk with God.

13

Jesus, His Son

. . . the blood of Jesus Christ his Son
(or, the blood of Jesus his Son) . . .

1 JOHN 1:7

It is the business of Christian preaching at all times, on all days and on all occasions, to be preaching Christ Jesus the Lord. But it is always good for us particularly and specially to remind ourselves of the facts and of the details lest we tend to assume we know them all, instead of constantly reminding ourselves of them. And here, in this one phrase, it seems to me we have a perfect account or epitome of the essential doctrine which is taught in the New Testament with regard to this great and vital subject—'the blood of Jesus his Son.'

Now these New Testament epistles were never written merely for the sake of writing; they were never produced merely as literary effusions of men who were fond of writing or whose vocation in life was that of producing literature. These letters came into being because of a situation that arose in the infant Christian Church; they were written with pastoral intent, and that is particularly true of this first epistle of John.

John is concerned, as we have seen all along, about the vital importance of understanding the doctrine concerning the person of our Lord Jesus Christ. This is, in a sense, the thing that made him write at all. As we go on through this epistle in subsequent volumes we shall find that he makes frequent references to what he calls 'anti-Christs', and he uses very strong language. He says that certain people who are writing about this doctrine are 'liars', and so according to John, it is very important that we should be perfectly clear, without any suspicion of doubt or of hesitation, with regard to the person of Jesus of Nazareth, the Son of God.

This is something that can never be emphasised too frequently; the whole case of the New Testament is bound up with this question. So it is something which we must constantly repeat, because it does seem to be the fatal tendency of mankind, even of the Christian Church herself, to divorce the teaching from the person. Yet the moment you do so, you have no real teaching. That is what differentiates this from everything else; it is not an idea or a proposal, nor is it a philosophy. It is the presentation of a person, without whom we have nothing at all.

I am not saying that there is no value at all in good, uplifting and moral teaching or that there is no benefit to be derived by society from the consideration of noble ideas and exalted conceptions with regard to life. That is all right, but it is just not Christianity. It has nothing to do with it, in a sense, and we can do no greater violence to the New Testament doctrine than to represent the message of Christ's birth[1] as but some vague general message of goodwill and of good cheer and happiness. That is not its message at all.

No, if we do not start with the person of the Lord Jesus Christ, if we are not absolutely clear about Him, then there is nothing. There is no good news, there is no evangel, there is no gospel; there is nothing to cheer us up, there is no hope. We are just living in the darkness of the world, and we are unutterably foolish in trying to persuade ourselves that things are better than they really are. There is no such thing, in a sense, as the 'Christmas spirit'. That is not the Christian message; it is not a vague spirit; it is a message of news concerning Him, so that, therefore, we must of necessity start at this point and be absolutely clear about this matter.

As has often been pointed out, 'Christianity is Christ'. It all centres round Him, and every doctrine that we have and every idea that we possess is something that comes from Him. Therefore, we must of necessity start with Him, and of course John in this letter has already done so. We pointed out, in dealing with the first three verses, that immediately he announced his message: 'That which was from the beginning, which we have heard, which we have seen with our eyes, which we have looked upon, and our hands have handled, of the Word of life . . . that which we have seen and heard declare we unto you.' He started at once with his doctrine, and it was the doctrine of the person. For the whole message which John has to deliver is, simply, that to us there is only one way of fellowship and communion with God, and that is because of the Lord Jesus Christ. It is He alone who can enable us to know this fellowship, for there is 'one mediator between God and men, the man Christ Jesus' (1 Tim 2:5).

So if He is the essential link, if He is the only way of communion with God, how vitally important it is that we should be perfectly clear about Him! And as we saw in those first three verses, John immediately proceeds to correct certain errors that had crept in with regard to His person, even in those early days. 'We have heard,' says John, 'we have seen with our eyes, we have looked upon, our hands have handled.' And there, immediately, he is correcting heresy. Indeed, as you look at this epistle and go through it, you are at once impressed by the great fact, which he goes on repeating, that it is these various doctrines with regard to the person of the Lord Jesus Christ that always tend to be the greatest source of trouble in the Christian Church. So we must be clear about this; otherwise we have nothing whatsoever.

So here in one phrase he again gives the whole doctrine, and to me there is nothing that is quite so wonderful or charming, in the true sense of the word, as the way in which so often in the Scriptures you have the whole of the doctrine put in a phrase like this. These men repeat it; they never apologise for that, they were always preaching the same theme; it was always this wonderful person. They never got far away from Him because He was everything to them, and so they go on repeating their whole doctrine, and here is a phrase which says it all–'the blood of Jesus his Son'.

What does this suggest to you? First of all it reminds us of the historical character of our faith. You see, our faith is concerned about the person of Jesus and there, immediately, we are in the realm of history. The Greek philosophers talk a great deal about their 'ideas'. These began as great ideas up in the heavens; then these great ideas had somehow or another become incarnate, but it was all in the realm of ideas. They were always concerned about thoughts, and so much that still passes as Christianity falls into that ancient error.

Now that is corrected here, because we are concerned about Jesus, 'Jesus his Son'; we are concerned about certain *facts*, and that is the great glory of our Christian faith, that it is something that is based upon a series of historical facts and events, and this very name, Jesus, reminds us of that. 'Jesus'–yes, the baby that was born in Bethlehem in a stable and placed in a manger; Jesus, an actual child that was born into this world; the boy Jesus arguing in the Temple, still right in the realm of history and of facts; a young man working as a carpenter, Jesus.

Then there were three years, the most amazing three years the world has ever known, when, having set out upon His public ministry, He travelled backwards and forwards, up and down that land of Palestine, preaching and teaching and working His miracles and dealing with the people. It is still solid history, yes, quite as definite as 55 B.C. when Julius Caesar conquered Britain; quite as real as 1066 and all other events of history–Jesus a person and all that we know about Him, culminating in the agony in the garden and on the cross and in the burial and the resurrection and the ascension.

Now that is what we are concerned about; it is as real, as realistic as that. Oh! how can one put this so that it may be clear to us once and for ever that we are essentially concerned about something that has taken place in history? When unbelievers or people who tell us that they are not Christians come to us and would have us believe that we are misled or that we have gone astray in believing our Christian faith and gospel, when they come and deny our truth and faith, the real answer to give them is not, 'You can say what you like, but I have felt or experienced something.' No, the real reply is history, the birth of the baby Jesus in the manger, and all the other facts that we have just mentioned.

Experience is not the ultimate proof of our Christian faith and its reality. Thank God, we do have experiences, but, thank God, we have something much more than that. With regard to experiences we must agree with the writer of the hymn who said, 'I dare not trust the sweetest frame'–feelings come and feelings go–

> *But wholly lean on Jesus' Name.*
> *On Christ, the solid Rock, I stand;*
> *All other ground is sinking sand.*
> Edward Mote

Jesus–the person, the one who has entered into history–thank God for a historical faith, thank God for a gospel that is based upon facts. That is the first thing that is suggested to us by this verse.

But let me go on to say a word about the wonder of the incarnation. Having looked in that way at the historicity of the incarnation, let us have a look at the wonder of it. Here, of course, the very words used by the Apostle, and especially these two words in juxtaposition, express the whole doctrine: '*Jesus his Son*'. What an amazing combination of words! You will find the writers of hymns sometimes invoking angels, sometimes wishing that they had the power and voice of an angel to express truth, and that is exactly how I feel as I take these words. Oh, for a thousand tongues to express it! Oh, for an angelic power of expression to bring out the full meaning of such terms, but here they are, put together.

The baby lying in the manger, His Son, God's Son. The boy aged twelve in the Temple reprimanded by Mary and Joseph for not having accompanied them as they went back from the feast at Jerusalem. Jesus–who is He? 'His Son', the Son of God. The carpenter working quietly day by day in His workshop, so much like others to all outward appearance and yet essentially different, doing His work and helping others–Jesus the carpenter of Nazareth? No–'Jesus his Son'. And on you go with the story, and all along it is the same.

What does all this convey to us? Well, here we are face to face with the whole marvel and wonder of the incarnation. The Apostle Paul puts it all in that grand passage of his in Philippians 2:5-11, which surely can never be improved upon: 'Let this mind be in you, which was also in Christ Jesus'–now here is the doctrine–'who, being in the form of God, thought it not robbery to be equal with God: but made himself of no reputation, and took upon him the form of a servant, and was made in the likeness of men; and being found in fashion as a man, he humbled himself, and became obedient unto death, even the death of the cross. Wherefore God hath highly exalted him, and given him a name which is above every name; that at the name of Jesus every knee should bow, of things in heaven, and things in earth, and things under the earth; and that every tongue should confess that Jesus Christ is Lord, to the glory of God the Father.'

But all that is really conveyed by this expression–'Jesus his Son'; the baby is none other than the Son of God. This involves all that Paul has put in that magnificent statement of his; it involves the humiliation of the incarnation; it involves what is there put as 'making himself of no reputation'; 'being in the form of God'–in other words having all the qualifications that make God God–having those essential things that are essential to deity, not an appearance but the thing itself in its essence. But how did one who was thus in the form of God become the baby lying in a manger? And the answer is that He did not hold on to, He did not clutch at all at the prerogatives and the insignia of deity to which he was thus entitled there in eternity; rather, He made Himself of no reputation. He did not cease to be God, He did not divest Himself of His deity; nor did He empty Himself of the content of eternity. No, that is error, that is heresy. But what He did was this: He decided that He would come on earth and not use them or employ them. He decided that He would, as it were, hold them in abeyance. He would live life as a man though He was still God–'Jesus his Son'.

We cannot understand this. It baffles not only the mind and understanding, but also the very imagination itself. But that is the picture that is conveyed of the marvel and the miracle of the incarnation in the New Testament. We have read at times of certain kings travelling incognito. The man is a king or a prince, but he does not let it be known; he lives as if he were an ordinary traveller. And it was something like that, multiplied by infinity, when the Son of God became Jesus. He did not use the powers, He did not exercise His prerogatives, He came in the likeness of man.

He came, indeed, in 'the likeness of sinful flesh' and He lived out His life as a man, but He was still God—God and man, God-man; two natures in one person and yet no co-mingling, not a kind of effusion of the two natures. No, two natures; still Jesus, yes, truly man, but all the time 'His Son', the unique Son of God, the one who has come out of the bosom of the Father. Two natures in one person and therefore that extraordinary person of whom we read in the Gospels and upon whom we meditate. This strange amazing thing—the baby in helplessness—Son of God; the boy with His understanding—Son of God; the carpenter—Son of God; always the two. Jesus, His Son.

Next let us see how this extraordinary phrase reminds us and establishes the reality of the incarnation: 'The blood of Jesus his Son.' Here John is again correcting those heresies that had crept in with regard to the person of our Lord. What he is really telling us in this phrase is that the incarnation does not mean that the Son of God took upon Him a phantom body. It is not that the Son of God put a kind of cloak or covering appearance of flesh and body. Not at all! 'The Word was made flesh' (Jn 1:14). He was not a spirit; this was not a theophany, a mere appearance. It is an *incarnation*—'a spirit hath not flesh and bones' (Lk 24:39); a spirit does not have blood, but it is 'the blood of Jesus his Son'. The incarnation is a reality; it is a fact.

Now there were certain people in that early Church to whom John had occasion to point out that particular heresy. They said that the Son of God could not really have been made flesh. 'It is impossible,' they said, 'for God to dwell on the earth as man and in the likeness of sinful flesh. No, what happened was this: when the eternal Son came on earth he took on this kind of phantom body, it was not a real one.' But John denies that when he says, 'the blood of Jesus'. The baby, the boy, the carpenter—it was an actual incarnation, not an appearance.

But let me put it like this also. There were those, you remember, who taught that Jesus certainly was a human being. They said they believed in the baby in a manger and the boy and so on, but what they tell us at this point is that at His baptism the eternal Christ entered into the man Jesus. 'There is no such thing as the virgin birth,' they said; 'there is no such thing as God actually being born and coming out of the virgin's womb. No, there, in the baptism, the eternal Christ somehow came into the man Jesus, and then He dwelt with Him throughout the three years, but on the cross left Him again. So that the Son of God did not die, it was Jesus the man who died'—that was actually being taught in the early Church.

It is good for us to remind ourselves that every single heresy that we can ever think of had been thought of probably before the end of the first century. There is nothing very modern or up to date in being heretical; it is as old as the gospel itself. Let no one think he is wonderful and modern in denying certain of these essential doctrines!

And this is John's reply: it is 'the blood of Jesus his Son' that cleanses us from all sin. The blood of man cannot do it, nor the blood of bulls and of goats. It was the very Son of God who died, as it was the Son of God who was born, as it was the Son of God who endured the contradiction of sinners against Himself and staggered up Golgotha. It was His blood that was shed. And that is the blood that purchased our pardon and forgiveness and reconciles us to God and opens the door of heaven to let us in. It is actual, it is real, it was not an appearance. The amazing doctrine is that as Jesus was the Son of God, it was the Son of God who died upon the cross. Wonder of wonders, marvel of marvels, even as He was dying, He was still Jesus, His Son, and it is that blood that sets us free.

There is one other deduction. We are reminded by this phrase of the whole purpose of the incarnation. Now the New Testament is never in any difficulty about this; its answer is always perfectly clear and plain and unequivocal. The Son of God was born as Jesus in Bethlehem in order that He might die. He came to die, and we should never speak of the incarnation except in terms of the death; all these doctrines are one and indissoluble. He came to taste death for every man; He came to die because nothing but that death could save us. That is the doctrine, so that as we think of 'the blood of Jesus his Son' we are reminded that nothing less, nothing else, could provide salvation.

God had given the law; God had sent His prophets and patriarchs. He had raised up great men and blessed them, and still there was no true salvation. The best men had failed; none could keep the law; 'every mouth [has been] stopped', 'the whole world [is] guilty before God', all have 'come short of the glory of God' (Rom 3:19, 23). Everything had been tried, and nothing was sufficient. There is only one way whereby man can be saved and reconciled to God; there must be a shedding of blood and a perfect offering and sacrifice. There must be someone who is man and yet more than man. He must be perfect and absolute.

So the Son of God came and took unto Himself human nature, and in this perfect human nature He shed His blood. And the Lord God is satisfied; the sacrifice and offering are perfect, and in Him God can forgive and pardon—'the blood of Jesus his Son.' The purpose of the incarnation is the death and the atonement, the resurrection and the reconciliation.

Last of all, how can we finish without considering, however feebly and unworthily, the love that led to all this. Just think of it; the Son of God, Jesus, the one through whom all things were made, the Word that is in the bosom of the Father, the Word that was God from the beginning, the eternal absolute Son enjoying all the full prerogatives of deity from everlasting to everlasting—lying helpless as a baby in a manger. And all that you and I might be saved and reconciled to God!

Oh, what wondrous love that should stoop so low! But look at the record, follow the story; look at Him suffering the scorn and the derision, the abuse, the jealousy, the envy, the hatred, the malice, the scourging. Look at Him as they put that heavy cross upon His holy shoulder. As He staggers beneath His load a man, Simon of Cyrene, has to come and help Him. Who is this struggling under this impossible weight? It is the everlasting eternal Son of God, Jesus, His Son! And why is He doing it? That you and I might be redeemed.

Look at Him there upon the cross, in His pain, suffering that agony that is almost unendurable. What does it all mean? Why has He done it all; why does He die; why does He suffer Himself to be buried in a grave? What has produced it all? And there is but one response—'Love, so amazing, so divine.'

God has come Himself in the person of the Son; He has known

that humiliation and the suffering and the contradiction of sinners and the agony and the shame, and He has done it so that we might be forgiven, that we might become His children and that we might go on to be with Him in glory for ever and ever. What amazing love, to give us so much, to stoop so low! 'God commendeth his love toward us, in that, while we were yet sinners, Christ died for us' (Rom 5:8).

'The blood of Jesus his Son!'

NOTES

CHAPTER FOUR: *The Apostolic Declaration*
1. The United Nations Association was an organisation set up in Britain after the Second World War to support the work of the United Nations.
2. Said in 1948 at the gathering of the World Council of Churches—he was accused of having 'thrown a bombshell into the proceedings'!

CHAPTER SIX: *All Because of Christ*
1. This sermon was preached on Remembrance Sunday 1948.

CHAPTER THIRTEEN: *Jesus, His Son*
1. This sermon was preached on 26th December 1948.